Sarah Dunant is a writer and bro[...] cultural journalist for twenty years working in radio and print, and is founding presenter BBC TV's *The Late Show*. The author of six novels, she lives in London with her two daughters.

UNIVERSITY OF GLAMORGAN
LEARNING RESOURCES CENTRE

Pontypridd, Mid Glamorgan, CF37 1DL
Telephone: Pontypridd (01443) 480480

Books are to be returned on or before the last date below

18 JUN 1996
18 MAR 1997
09 JUN 1998
-9 NOV 1999
-7 DEC 1999
14 JAN 2000
14 JAN 2000
-5 MAY 2000
28 SEP 2001
13 JAN 2006
21 FEB 2006
27 MAR 2006
09 JAN 2009
14 DEC 2009
08 JAN 2010

THE WAR OF THE WORDS

The Political Correctness Debate

edited by
SARAH DUNANT

1096473 8 306 WAR

1853818348

Published by VIRAGO PRESS Limited October 1994
42–43 Gloucester Crescent, Camden Town, London NW1 7PD

Copyright © Sarah Dunant 1994
Copyright © for each contribution is held by the author 1994

All rights reserved

The right of Sarah Dunant to be identified as the editor of this work has been asserted by her in accordance with the Copyright, Designs and Patents Act 1988

A CIP catalogue record for this book is available from the British Library

Printed in Britain by Cox & Wyman Ltd., Reading, Berks.

8.6.95

Contents

Acknowledgements

Much thanks and admiration to all the writers in this book who went into battle over the meanings and ideas within PC and whose arguments have produced such a challenging debate. And to Lennie Goodings at Virago without whom this book would not exist.

Introduction

WHAT'S IN A WORD?

PC is a dirty word in nineties Britain. To call someone PC is less a description than an insult, carrying with it accusations of everything from Stalinism/McCarthyism to (even worse?) having no sense of humour. It is also a convenient stick to beat all number of backs with. Junior government ministers use it to explain why so many women are bringing up children without fathers. Prince Charles thinks it's the reason why certain parents won't smack their children. And the tabloids – well, the tabloids see it as everything from the social worker who sacks a child minder because she keeps a golliwog as a toy, to women who refuse to wear the kind of bras that give them extra uplift.

At a more apocalyptic level political correctness is hailed as a movement which, if allowed to run unchecked, will curtail free speech, deny common sense, threaten the foundations of family life and rewrite our literary and national histories until all notions of western values are denied.

The problem with all this hysteria is that it is not only open to the same charge levelled at PC itself – that of the misuse of language (to call PC warriors Red Guards or Hitler Youth is simply inaccurate and misleading) – but that it makes any kind of genuine debate about the pros and cons of what political correctness is, and stands for, almost impossible.

This book of essays is an attempt to address the problem, to get behind the tabloid headlines and the insults and take a sane, critical and long overdue look at what PC actually is, where it came from and what its aims and methods are. How much is it to be feared or welcomed? How does it fit into the political landscape of our times? And, perhaps most important of all, how far within that landscape does it represent a critical moment for the future of the left in Britain?

The phenomenon of political correctness as it is defined today grew out of the American campuses in the mid-to-late 1980s. Focused largely on the arts and humanities faculties, it was an attempt to open up the literary canon to include the work of more non-white and women writers, to rethink the ways in which history was taught and to promote sexual and racial equality by means of certain kinds of positive discrimination and, in some cases, speech and behaviour codes on campus. With its overtones of enforcing tolerance and prescribing behaviour it was perhaps inevitable that PC should lead to such absurdities as the Antioch College code of sexual behaviour which insisted on verbal agreement before any and every stage of sexual courtship, and to accusations that Andrew Marvell's ode 'To his Coy Mistress' was simply a sophisticated piece of sexual harassment. Even allowing for the mischief of the media in equating these extremes with the mainstream, American PC, with its flamboyant, apparently OTT methods, might seem to have little to do with us on the other side of the Atlantic.

But those who dismiss PC as just a storm in an American Academic tea cup are wrong. Because of the importance of the campus in America (nearly 50 per cent of all Americans go to college) what happens there has an impact on the rest of the country. The PC debate is news. There are now enough books and essays on it to support its own master's thesis. But this is not simply an academic issue. It is, as John Annette documents in his opening essay, also a political one. Because at root PC is about more than equality or tolerance. It is about power, who has it and what they do with it. With America in the grip of a sustained period of right wing government, preaching aggressive free market economics and reduced government welfare, issues of race and gender (issues always associated with the left) had been more or less knocked off the political agenda. PC, both on and off campus, has helped to put them back on. One has only to look at the number of times commentators now seek to define the Clinton administration – particularly Hillary Clinton's part within it – as 'PC' to show how far the word has become party political now.

So what has all this to do with us? Well, quite a lot actually. While many commentators here were denouncing the arrival of PC as some dread American import, as damaging to our culture as McDonald's has been to our taste buds, the fact is that its concerns – the promotion of rights and sensibilities of racial and sexual minorities through education, positive discrimination and culture – had already been part of a limited, but nevertheless bloody, political skirmish fought here during the early 1980s in the arena of the Greater London Council and other Labour run local councils. Of course there were differences of ideology and strategy between Ken Livingstone's GLC and 1990s PC – though you'd be hard pressed to tell that from the media reports. Take almost any recent tabloid PC headline, substitute the words 'loony left' for 'PC' and I guarantee you'll not be able to tell whether the story came from 1994 or '84.

It's now almost ten years since any political challenge posed by the GLC was quashed through its abolition, but it's true to say that in certain key areas, in debates about social work and education for instance, its ideological legacy lives on. Indeed one of the unexpected things that emerges from this set of essays is a reassessment of the political and cultural impact of the GLC.

Similarities between the GLC here and PC in America are, in the end though, perhaps not that surprising. The two countries may have different breakdowns in terms of ethnic and race divisions but, broadly speaking, the political impetus towards issues of sexual and racial equality in both grew out of the same cultural and political liberal philosophies of the 1960s. Philosophies which here, as well as there, have found themselves under sustained political siege during the last fifteen years and which, denied access to central government, have developed and re-emerged wherever there has been an opportunity; in Britain through the power of local government and in America with the rise of the sixties generation to positions of greater importance within the academic hierarchy.

But there is one respect in which PC has, in political terms, gone a good deal further. Because although the theatrical and sometimes confrontational character of the GLC did cause a certain amount of embarrassment among the parliamentary left in Britain at the time, it is nothing to the kind of panic button that PC has pushed a decade later.

What PC has done is achieve the remarkable double whammy of offending both the right and a good deal of the left at the same time. In terms of the right this alienation was inevitable. In terms of the left however, as a number of the essays in this book show, it has been a more complex and tragic affair. The problem is less with the aims of PC than with its methods (although commentators like Melanie Phillips would argue that the two were always inexorably intertwined).

For many liberals a movement which claimed to be about opening up the culture to allow more voices in has, instead, only succeeded in alienating voices that were already there. What price more women and black writers in the canon if that means the exclusion of other equally brilliant and historically important white male ones? What price racial and sexual equality if it can only be achieved by the imposition of another set of rules, in some cases amounting to what many see as a direct censorship of speech or behaviour? You don't achieve freedom by being frightened of what you can and can't say. That way lies intolerance, rather than the opposite.

Free speech was one of the rocks on which sixties liberalism built its church. Another was sexual freedom; that men and women should be allowed to go to bed with each other (in whatever combination) without interference from the state or any other form of authority. Although it's easy to understand where it is coming from, the kind of sexual anxieties and proscriptions that Katie Roiphe describes as the new campus feminism in her book *The Morning After* sends a shiver of fear down the liberal spine. As she puts it – what price sexual freedom if it means we end up behaving like our grandmothers?

All these examples are, of course, just that: instances or stories picked up and, some would say, misrepresented or blown out of all proportion just to make a point. Indeed, just how far PC's methods really are, well, as PC as some people claim them to be, is one of the underlying questions addressed in this book, by both its supporters and its detractors.

But whatever the claims and counterclaims, PC has caused a Richter scale tremor within the liberal conscience. With its emphasis on the rights and demands of minorities, it is often cited as one of the guilty parties in the growth of what has become known as victim culture. The great fear about victim culture is the effect it will have: that the cacophony of voices demanding attention will, far from achieving a richer cultural mix, only succeed in breaking apart any notion of a cultural whole. This idea of cultural fragmentation (in itself a potent bogeyman of post-modernism) is one of the things that opponents of political correctness always return to. It is the central thesis of Robert Hughes' *Culture of Complaint*, the celebrated critique of both right and left American PC, which acts as the starting point for Christopher Hitchens' essay about what he sees as the dangers of PC for American society.

But Hitchens' is only one of a number of voices in *The War of the Words*. There are others who do not agree with him. In fact, the ten essayists divide almost down the middle in either supporting or opposing PC (some doing both at the same time). Any dinner table which included them all would, you feel, end with more than just words flying. While Hitchens denounces an ideology that he sees as undermining free speech ('I did not come to America to watch what I say'), linguist Deborah Cameron defiantly argues the reasons why PC *must* challenge and alter language in order to effect change. Journalists Melanie Phillips and Yasmin Alibhai-Brown slug it out on opposite sides of the great liberal divide, in passionate disagreement as to whether PC is a political and cultural aberration, betraying all that liberalism stands for (Melanie Phillips), or a long overdue force for change which has exposed a hypocrisy at the heart of a liberalism only willing to incorporate demands of equality when those demands don't threaten its own innate sense of privilege (Yasmin Alibhai-Brown).

Assessing the impact of PC on the campus and the curriculum, John Annette concludes that in America, behind all the sound and fury, it has been neither as apocalyptic nor as pervasive as its right wing critics would have us believe, while Lisa Jardine talks about the curriculum she teaches here in Britain, one which although it would never actively seek to exclude the likes of Philip Larkin might, over time – given his views of race and sexual politics – effectively see Larking marginalising himself.

Actress and scriptwriter Meera Syal describes how the British version of PC gave her the opportunities and confidence not just to become a writer, but to say things that were controversial even within her own community. Linda Grant considers the contentious topic of date rape, exploring the alliance of PC and feminism on campus and changing attitudes towards rape over the last generation, while Lisa Appignanesi analyses PC from the standpoint of French culture, asking why, despite sexual and racial inequalities and tensions in France, the movement has gained no foothold there.

Stuart Hall's essay, which ends the book, puts political correctness in the broader historical and political context. Analysing its failures and its strengths, he argues that the left here in Britain had better learn from both if it's going to reconstruct itself as any kind of credible and effective political force for the future.

That observation – and Hall is not the only one to make it, it runs through the book like an underground current – is crucial. This is a critical moment for the left in Britain. With the government in severe political disarray, the way in which the left now fights for and – should it be successful – uses power could determine our political and moral landscape well into the next century. Whatever you might think of PC, the issues it addresses are going to make up a large part of that landscape. With the evils of nationalism and ethnic cleansing once again inside the borders of Europe, the idea of Britain as a genuinely multicultural society where all the voices are included and protected may sound like liberal cliché, but it could also become political necessity. While in a country where fewer than a quarter of us live in the back-to-basics fairy tale of the traditional nuclear family, the changing relationship of men and women, economically, sexually and emotionally, throws up moral and political questions that cannot be ignored. For those reasons, though PC may not be the right blueprint for a way forward, it demands a good deal more serious consideration than the dismissive insult or the trivial headline.

The War of the Words, I hope, provides that. I would like to think it might leave the reader a little mentally challenged. You can make up your own mind as to the meaning of that phrase.

Sarah Dunant, April 1994

John Annette

THE CULTURE WARS ON THE AMERICAN CAMPUS

In the early 1990s, the American media began to sensationalise the issue of political correctness on the campuses of the universities of the United States. 'Are you politically correct?' was the title of an article in the *New York Magazine* (21 January 1991) in which a full page photomontage juxtaposed an image of young Nazis burning books in the 1930s with one of Red Guards parading the enemies of the Maoist cultural revolution. According to the magazine, political correctness was a 'new fundamentalism' threatening individual freedoms, especially freedom of speech. The new fundamentalists were 'an eclectic group; they include multiculturalists, feminists, radical homosexuals, Marxists, New Historicists. What unites them . . . is their conviction that Western culture and American society are thoroughly and hopelessly racist, sexist and oppressive.'

Later in the year, Dinesh D'Souza's conservative book *Illiberal Education: The Politics of Race and Sex on Campus*[1] hit the bestseller list and he became a media celebrity. The stakes were raised even further on 4 May 1991 when President George Bush (soon to seek re-election) gave a speech at the University of Michigan in which he defended free speech against the new McCarthyism of political correctness. 'PC' had become a national policy issue.

But what is it? According to both its right and left critics it represents a form of Orwellian thought police on the campus exercising power and surveillance both explicitly and implicitly. Some commentators see political correctness as a conspiracy of 1960s radicals who are not only subverting the teaching of the canon of Western culture, in the name of feminism and multiculturalism, but are also denying free speech by institutionalising speech codes and codes of behaviour in order to eliminate racism, sexism, homophobia, etc. The issue of political correctness, I believe, importantly reflects not only a crisis within the academy but also a growing unease about the direction in which many see American society moving.

With hindsight it is not surprising that the issue of political correctness and the crisis of the academy began during the years of the Reagan–Bush presidency. Having already attacked 'card-carrying liberals' who administered social welfare, the new right now extended their ideological crusade by presenting new left academics as dangerous radicals who were undermining higher education by politicising it. They began to champion the ideal of the disinterested pursuit of truth. Lynne Cheney, a leading new right academic and the chair of the National Endowment for the Humanities, a powerful public funding body, wrote that 'the Humanities are about more than politics, about more than social power. What gives them their abiding worth are truths that pass beyond time and circumstance; truths that, transcending class, race and gender, speak to us all.'[2] Ironically, this disingenuous attempt to depoliticise learning only succeeded in further fuelling the politicisation of the debate about the purpose of higher education.

While liberal academics may see the attack on political correctness as merely an hysterical media creation, there is no doubt that it touches some of America's deepest concerns – on both the right and the left. Not just about the curriculum and the issues of racism, sexism and homophobia on campus but also about the admission and recruitment of students, the decline of academic standards and the increasing of tuition fees and crisis of funding. There is certainly a growing loss of confidence in one of the world's largest and best-funded collection of universities. However, what is less clear is the extent to which the sensational image of political correctness represents accurately what is actually happening on campus.

Sometimes it seems it's all in the interpretation. One of the best-known early examples of a threat to academic freedom, cited to back the charge that a new McCarthyism was sweeping universities, is the case of the liberal democrat and pioneering historian of race and immigration,

Professor Stephen Thernstrom of Harvard University. For several years Thernstrom, along with Pulitzer prize-winning historian Bernard Bailyn, taught a course on the history of race relations in the United States. In autumn 1987 the student newspaper began to print articles which accused Bailyn and especially Thernstrom of racial insensitivity. Students complained that the voices of the slaves themselves were not represented in the course materials in his history of slavery. Professor Thernstrom claimed that such material was not available for teaching. When students, reluctantly, came forward to make formal complaints, they were taken up by the Committee on Race Relations set up by the university president, Derek Bok, a leading figure in higher education. At the same time the Dean of the college issued an open letter to the Harvard community, warning against racial harassment. According to Dinesh D'Souza, this was a clear-cut example of a good liberal professor hounded by his students and unsupported in his academic freedom by his university authorities. On the other hand, an account by Jon Weiner in the *Nation* presented it merely as a disagreement.[3] He claimed that the Committee on Race Relations refused to hear the case until the students talked it out with their professor and that when they did both parties agreed to disagree and no further action was taken. However, Professor Thernstrom himself felt compelled to drop his controversial course ('it just isn't worth it', he said) and saw himself as a victim of McCarthyism.

Let us consider the use of the term McCarthyism, which is regularly deployed in the PC debate. Under the influence of McCarthyism in the 1950s, large numbers of academics were prevented by the government from teaching and received little or no support from university administrators. There is no evidence that any academics today have been prevented from teaching or have been dismissed by the administration because of their perceived political views. Like students on the left who continually cry fascist when confronting university administrators, the new right critics devalue the powerful meaning of the term McCarthyism.

However, there is evidence that a growing number of academics on both the left and the right are facing criticism from students and colleagues because of their attitudes towards, among other issues, racism, sexism and ethnicity and perhaps find themselves exercising self-censorship or meeting peer group pressure. As a result, academic freedom has become an important part of the national debate about political correctness for university teachers.

In 1987 the National Association of Scholars was established to defend academic freedom and to reappraise critically PC doctrines such as affirmative action and campus speech and behaviour censorship. In opposition, a number of leading liberal academics established in 1991 the Teachers for a Democratic Culture. In their Statement of Principles, they decry the hypocrisy of those who claim to be above politics at the same time as criticising the politicisation of higher education. They also point out the power base of the criticism, coming as it does from such wealthy institutions as the American Enterprise Institute, the Olin Foundation and the public National Endowment for the Humanities, etc. One of the main attacks lobbed in return at the Teachers for a Democratic Culture is the conspiracy-of-1960s-radicals-now-in-positions-of-power theory.

In his book *Tenured Radicals*,[4] the managing editor of

the conservative cultural journal the *New Criterion*, Roger Kimball, argues that 'it's important to appreciate the extent to which the radical vision of the sixties has not so much been abandoned as internalised by many who came of age then and who teach at and administer our institutions of higher education'. In this provocative book, in the spirit of free speech, he 'names the names' of academics whom he sees as representing this academic new left. Dinesh D'Souza agrees with this conspiracy of radicals theory and in his book went on to give examples of 'thought police' at such well-known institutions as the University of California at Berkeley, Duke, Howard, Michigan and Stanford Universities. The new right critics also cite university administrators involved in cases of affirmative action admission policies or campus speech codes along with student radicals in order to provide evidence that a new radicalism is plaguing the nation's campuses.

One of the interesting – some would say challenging – aspects about the political correctness debate is the shifting meanings and alliances of left and right. For example, Professor Stanley Fish, author of *There's No Such Thing as Free Speech . . . and it's a good thing too*,[5] is often referred to as a leading symbolic figure of this culture war. Because he is an original and iconoclastic critic of both the right and the left he defies a crude classification as a left academic. Another example is Professor Eugene Genovese, a well-known Marxist historian, who praised D'Souza's book and called political correctness a new barbarism. But while most new right critics are unified in their view of the cause and meaning of 'politically correct nonsense', the debate has greatly divided the left. It is interesting to note that the entry of new left intellectuals into positions of power in the university in the 1970s is seen by some radicals as leading to the demise of the cultural critic who previously wrote for a public audience but is now assimilated by the university. Yet the debate about political correctness seems to me to illustrate the fact that many academics are concerned to address major political issues and to reach out to a wider audience by responding to significant cultural and political changes in American society but at the same time are reluctant to politicise the academy itself.

One of the first shots in the culture war was the phenomenally bestselling book *The Closing of the American Mind* by the late Allan Bloom.[6] A profoundly conservative book, it represents the influence of the ideas and charismatic teaching of Leo Strauss who saw the study of the 'Great Tradition' as a window to the knowledge of universal truths and values and saw modernity as leading to relativism, historicism and the crisis of the West. Strauss's writings were probably too esoteric for the general public, indeed, he believed that philosophy must remain the preserve of an intellectual minority. Yet he influenced a large number of academics in America and Allan Bloom was certainly one of his main disciples. Bloom's view of knowledge as the disinterested pursuit of truth identified German idealism and especially the writings of Nietzsche and Heidegger as undermining learning in American universities by introducing the ideas of cultural relativism. While most readers of Bloom would have bought the book because of its scathing attack on contemporary youth culture, it did help to establish the public's view that something called post-modernism or post-structuralism or, even more specifically, deconstruction theory undermined Western rationality and belief in liberalism. Theorists like Jacques Derrida, Michel Foucault and Jacques Lacan are just some of the key writers who have been demonised as subverting the American university curriculum. It is also true, however, that many leading American post-structuralist philosophers, like Richard Rorty and more radically Cornell West, believe the ideas of cultural relativism and historicism are to be found in the philosophy of the American pragmatists, like John Dewey, and provide the basis for a more democratic approach to teaching and university reform.

Whatever the philosophical origins of cultural relativism might be, it seems to me that the electoral failure of democratic liberalism, the poor success rate of the 1960s social action programmes and even the collapse of Marxist politics have turned radical politics increasing towards identity politics or what is called the politics of difference. The politics of class action or liberal reformism gave way in the 1980s to a politics which classified people according to race, ethnicity and gender. Increasingly, multiculturalism and feminism became the main political agenda of university politics. The post-modernist analysis that sees all knowledge as political and shaped by competing forms of discourse or language provided an intellectual framework in which the politics of identity developed.

As a result the political ordering of knowledge and the teaching of the core undergraduate curriculum has become a national political issue. One of the best known controversies was at Stanford University where the debate over the replacement of a series of courses in Western Culture with ones in Cultures, Ideas and Values led to a campaign on campus saw students chanting 'Hey, hey, ho, ho, Western culture's got to go' and attacking students and staff on the teaching of DWEM (Dead White European Males). The more intellectual debate centred on anthropological arguments for studying diverse and past cultures. When the dust settled the bulk of the courses at Stanford remained unaltered and new texts were included rather than 'classic texts' excluded. The view that the teaching of the liberal arts curriculum has been substantially altered by advocates for PC is much exaggerated. The truth is that studies in 1986 and 1990 by the Modern Language Association (the professional body of English Literature academics) show that the basic core subjects are still being taught, that established authors are still being studied and that, while new courses in, for example, women's literature and Black American literature are being introduced, significantly, they are not part of the core curriculum. Shakespeare, much more than Alice Walker, is still required reading for undergraduates in English in American universities, contrary to what D'Souza would have us believe.

From today's perspective it looks as though the curriculum is the new battleground. Although it may be true that the rival claims of racial, ethnic and sexual identity fill the void left by the absence of any larger community identity, the fact is that the curriculum has long been the object of political academic debate. From the late nineteenth century, when the traditional classical curriculum was deposed by a flexible elective (modular) system at Harvard, to the introduction during the First World War of the Western civilisation courses (which were seen as justifying the war effort by depicting a struggle between civilisation and barbarism), the curriculum has always been a political battlefield. By the 1930s the teaching of Western civilisation courses had spread to many American universities and had become a progressive history which emphasised the European origins of American cultural identity. The current conflict over the Western canon and Western civilisation courses is just another chapter in the political history of the American university curriculum.

What do today's warring groups actually hope to win? Traditionalists might hope to hold on to a curriculum of classic texts written by great thinkers (or Dead White European Males). Liberals might hope to add key representative texts by women and by writers from different racial and ethnic groups, while radicals might hope to overthrow the whole canon and replace it with texts that represent the cultural politics of contemporary American society. But the very existence of this conflict provides the opportunity to revitalise American higher education. By engaging colleagues and students in debating how one teaches the core curriculum, Gerald Graff in his book, *Beyond the Culture Wars*,[7] hopes to encourage students to make better sense of their education. Yet questions about the meaning and importance of the overall undergraduate curriculum are rarely the main concerns of either students or staff. A major study of universities, the Carnegie Commission on the Undergraduate Experience in America, found that most academics, like many students, saw themselves as members of a community of convenience. The eighteenth- and nineteenth-century ideal of an academic community sharing a common view of education was already an anachronism by the early twentieth century. In fact, in a mass system of higher education a key problem is simply to get staff and students to participate in the debate about the whole purpose of higher education.

This is not to say the conflict on campus that the media has highlighted does not exist. The politics of identity has led to a sense of conflict on many campuses where there is an increase in racial, ethnic and sexual harassment, a growing racial and ethnic separatism and the introduction of speech and behaviour codes. The most famous example of a code of behaviour cited by the defenders of free speech was the one introduced in 1988 at the University of Michigan which prohibited any victimisation on grounds of 'race, ethnicity, religion, sex, sexual orientation, creed, national origin, ancestry, age, marital status, handicap or Vietnam-era veteran status'. The American Civil Liberties Union challenged the University of Michigan's violation of the First Amendment (free speech) and the US District Court struck down the Michigan code as unconstitutional. Despite this, however, several universities have introduced restrictive policies since then and the issue of free speech continues to be a heated one. Radical intellectuals like Stanley Fish look critically at the established liberal claim for free speech and argue that the law guaranteeing it has always been subject to political interpretation. In America where there is a powerful culture of rights there is a need for a common political language that recognises basic individual rights while providing a shared moral vocabulary.

The changing politics of multiculturalism and feminism on campus reflects the fact that the university is in some ways a microcosm of American society. In 1988 there were 10.3 million white, 1.1 million Afro-American, 680,000 Hispanic, 497,000 Asian American and 93,000 foreign students enrolled in American colleges. The United States is rapidly becoming a multicultural society as immigration from Latin America, the Caribbean and Asia changes the racial and ethnic composition of the population. The transformation of the American university since the 1960s involved a shift from what were traditional male and white colleges to the situation today where some 55 per cent of students are women and almost 20 per cent are non-white or Hispanic. More recently the critical situation of young Afro-American males who are in frightening numbers sliding into unemployment and crime is reflected in the decrease in their numbers entering into higher education. Affirmative action programmes, though seen by many liberals and conservatives as unjust, illustrate how academics attempt to use the university to promote equality. The politics of identity has also created the problem of racial, ethnic and sexual separatism and fragmentation and has led to a new politics of victimhood. While, according to journalist and political commentator Barbara Ehrenreich, 'verbal uplift is not the revolution', it is also true that a multicultural curriculum and protection from racial and sexual harassment do not provide the basis for achieving equal opportunity.

While conservatives see multiculturalism and feminism as dangerously leading to the denial of a common American identity, they interestingly share with many liberals and Marxists a concern about cultural fragmentation and racial and ethnic separatism. In an age of volatile racial and ethnic conflict from Brooklyn to Los Angeles, these are crucially important political issues. The politics of multicultural identity is double-edged, in that while it is potentially more unstable and open to ethnocentrism and separatism, it can also be, for example, in the writings of a leading African American studies scholar like Henry Louis Gates Jr,[8] both pluralist and democratic. On campus there is also now a debate about feminism and sexuality which looks critically at the issues of the politics of victimhood, heterosexuality, and the complicated and worrying issue of date rape. The debate about political correctness, though deeply divisive, creates an important opportunity to examine how universities might provide a higher education that helps American society to adapt to some of the fundamental social and political changes it faces.

Although the ideal of a common American cultural identity may be a myth or a mosaic based on a series of mythologies, some shared political vision is essential for social cohesion. A political vision based on the traditional American ideals of liberty, equality and democracy which also recognises social diversity must be at the centre of any debate about the purpose and future of higher education. This is true not only in the United States but also in Britain where the number of students is increasing dramatically, and universities and colleges are beginning to face the challenge of providing a quality and socially meaningful education for a mass public.

NOTES

1 Free Press, 1991.
2 *Humanities in America: A Report to the President, the Congress and the American People*, National Endowment for the Humanities, 1988.
3 30 September 1991.
4 *Tenured Radicals: How Politics Has Corrupted Higher Education*, Harper & Row, 1990.
5 OUP, 1994.
6 *The Closing of the American Mind: How Higher Education Has Failed Democracy and Impoverished the Souls of Today's Students*, Simon & Schuster, 1987.
7 *Beyond the Culture Wars: How Teaching the Conflicts Can Revitalise American Education*, W. Norton, 1993.
8 *Loose Canons: Notes on the Cultural Wars*, OUP, 1994.

Other key books include: Arthur M. Schlesinger, Jr, *The Disuniting of America: Reflections on a Multicultural Society*, W. Norton, 1992; David Bromwich, *Politics By Other Means*, Yale UP, 1992; Robert Hughes, *Culture of Complaint: The Fraying of America*, OUP, 1993. In addition, selections from some of the important articles, interviews, etc., can be found in Paul Berman (ed.), *Debating PC: The Controversy Over Political Correctness on College Campuses*, Dell, 1992, Patricia Aufderheide (ed.), *Beyond PC: Towards a Politics of Understanding*, Graywolf Press, 1992, and Darryl Gless and Barbara Herrnstein Smith (eds), *The Politics of Liberal Education*, Duke UP, 1992.

Deborah Cameron

'WORDS, WORDS, WORDS': THE POWER OF LANGUAGE

In the 1980s, a New York feminist friend of mine had a T-shirt bearing the slogan 'Politically Incorrect'. Recently she threw it out: there was, she explained, only a brief cultural moment when its intended message – something like, 'I am committed to leftist/feminist causes, but not humourless or doctrinaire about it' – was likely to be understood. That moment had already passed when in 1991 the now celebrated article by John Taylor in *New York Magazine* inquired: 'Are you politically correct?'[1] By then, the seemingly straightforward yes/no question put people like my friend with the T-shirt in a double bind. To say yes was to claim for yourself a definition constructed by conservatives for the express purpose of discrediting you; to say no was to place yourself among those conservatives.

Like the classic example sentence illustrating presupposition in semantics textbooks, 'The King of France is bald', 'Are you politically correct?' depends on a false or contested proposition (that there is a King of France, or that 'political correctness' refers to a real phenomenon with such-and-such characteristics). To answer it at all is to accept the questioner's presupposition when what you really want to do is challenge it. That, of course, takes a lot more space than is available on the average T-shirt.

Whether 'political correctness' really does refer to an entity in the world is open to question, but it is undoubtedly an item in the lexicon of our language. The way right-wing commentators have established certain presuppositions about it is a triumph – as a sociolinguist I can only admire it – of the politics of definition, of linguistic intervention. 'PC' now has such negative connotations for so many people, the mere invocation of the phrase can move those so labelled to elaborate disclaimers, or reduce them to silence (as another American friend drily observed, in some circles nowadays it's a case of 'you say PC when you used to say CP'). There is a certain irony in this, given that among the main charges against the so-called 'politically correct' are on one hand that they are abusing language, and on the other that by privileging 'trivial' questions of language they are moving away from real politics into a world where it seems to matter more what you call things than whether you can do anything about them.

The same charges could be easily levelled against the opposing camp; conservatives have deliberately set out to redefine the term 'political correctness', and they have also put considerable effort into disseminating some of their own nomenclatural variants (including for instance the charming coinage 'feminazi'). But to talk about 'charges', as if attempts to intervene in language were somehow illegitimate, is really to miss the point I want to pursue here. Put crudely, the point is this: in an age of mass communications, T-shirt slogans and soundbites, the politics of language (more generally, of definition and representation) has taken on a new importance. This development seems to baffle conservatives and liberals alike, and the tenor of recent public discourse about it suggests its implications have not yet been grasped. I want to try to bring out what is at stake when people argue about what to call things, and to place our current wars of words in some kind of perspective.

Anyone familiar with the history of English will know there is nothing new in arguments about the use of words: politically motivated campaigns for linguistic reform are not just a bizarre invention of the last decade. (Even that most modern of irritants, the Great Generic Pronoun Controversy, was raised in parliament by John Stuart Mill almost 150 years ago.) So far as I know, there has never been a time when people were content merely to speak their language, and not in addition to speak *about* it; there has never been a culture which did not believe that some ways of using words were functionally, aesthetically or morally preferable to others – though equally there has never been one that did not violently disagree about which ways these were.

Our capacity for reflecting on language and our tendency to make value judgements on it lead to the phenomenon of 'verbal hygiene' – a set of practices whose object is to 'clean up' the language, whether by upholding its supposed traditions (the project, for instance, of recent revisions to the English national curriculum) or by proposing wholesale improvements (the project of spelling reformers, Esperantists and of the so-called 'politically correct'). Where the underlying values informing such projects are contested, the verbal hygiene practices that seek to express those values in rules about language use will also be contested.

Although there are exceptions, in general it has been true that conservatives have practised verbal hygiene with a view to upholding tradition (or what they idealised as tradition), whereas liberals have practised forms of verbal hygiene more in line with their enlightened belief in rationality, progress, the perfectibility of humankind and human institutions. One novel thing about so-called 'political correctness' is that the parties do not line up in quite the expected way. Furthermore, much of the debate is being conducted in arenas – the mass media – which have sociolinguistic effects of their own. The complications are aptly illustrated in the history of the term 'political correctness' itself.

The terms 'politically correct' and 'politically incorrect' can be traced to the countercultural movements of the American new left in the late 1960s and 1970s. According to Ruth Perry's article 'A short history of the term *politically correct*',[2] the source from which these groups adopted the phrase was probably the English translation of Mao's *Little Red Book*. Alternatively, Barbara Epstein has suggested a connection with 'correct lineism',[3] a term used in the Communist Party.

The earliest print citation Perry found for 'politically correct' occurs in a 1970 article by the writer Toni Cade, which included the statement 'a man cannot be politically correct and a chauvinist too'. Although Cade was using the term straightforwardly, to argue that sexism had no place in radical Black politics, Ruth Perry points out that this was not the only way the term was used, and as time went on it became less and less the dominant way of using it. The most common use of 'politically correct' was *ironic* – to quote Maurice Isserman, writing in the progressive Jewish magazine *Tikkun* in 1991, 'it was always used in a tone mocking the pieties of our own insular political counterculture, as in "we could stop at McDonald's down the road if you're hungry . . . but it wouldn't be *politically correct*"'. This 'mocking' tone also attached to the Communist Party's 'correct lineism': a 'correct lineist' was a comrade whose holier-than-thou espousal of party dogma made other comrades want to spit.

The terms 'politically correct' and 'politically incorrect' were used as in-group markers and understood by insiders as a joke at their own expense. They functioned on one hand to differentiate the new left from the orthodox old left, and on the other to satirise the ever-present tendency of 'politicos' to become over-earnest, humourless and rigidly prescriptive, poking fun at the notion that anyone could be (or would want to be) wholly 'correct'. The meaning of these terms on the left, then, was an ironic mirror image of the one now attributed to them by the right.

It is, however, that attributed meaning which is the starting point for the current debate on 'political correctness'. The ascendency of the noun phrase ('political correct*ness*') over the adjective is notable in itself; not only can I, as a late 1970s vintage feminist and socialist, recall few non-ironic uses of 'politically correct' (or its preferred equivalent in Britain, 'ideologically sound'), I cannot recall the nominalisation with 'correctness', which has the effect of implying the existence of a referent, being in my vocabulary at all. That is why I keep alluding to 'so-called' political correctness and putting the term itself in scare-quotes: 'political correctness' has come to be used in a sense defined entirely by its self-proclaimed opponents.

To the extent that discussion of it is carried on in and through mass media, an additional factor comes into play which might be called 'discursive drift'. For most people, who have not been involved in a radical political subculture on either the left or the right, 'political correctness' and related terms are neologisms whose meaning must be inferred from context. Mass media can spread such newly coined words more widely and more quickly than either face-to-face communication or elite forms of writing, but the context they provide is insufficient to guarantee an exact transfer of meaning: they do not engage in the tedious definitions one finds in scholarly journals, and there is no opportunity for the addressee to ask for clarification, as happens in face-to-face talk. People may thus arrive at all kinds of inferences about the meaning of a new term they encounter in the media, and as they start to use it in other contexts themselves, it begins to drift away from the particular sense it had for those whose discussions were the original subject of media comment. (This is the same process that has made 'gender' into a polite synonym for 'sex' – the very term it was meant to contrast with – so that people now inquire about the 'gender' of cats and dogs.)

At the beginning of the present debate on 'political correctness' in the US around 1987, the term was used in connection with a specific set of issues to do with the university. The agitation around these issues led to some bestselling books and newsworthy incidents which were widely reported on both sides of the Atlantic. This meant that many people were introduced to the term 'political correctness' who had no connection with the university debate, and whose interpretations were informed only by the less richly contextualised reporting of it in the media.

Many people who encountered the term in this way appear to have drawn the inference that 'political correctness' meant something like, 'paying any kind of attention whatsoever to gender or race'. The term began to emerge in contexts where its use would previously have seemed both odd and unnecessary: for example, the British Methodist Conference of 1992 narrowly defeated a proposal to make 'balanced-gender' liturgy mandatory after the Reverend Roger Ducker made a speech in which he said: 'I very much fear there is a sort of thought police imposing a political correctness'.[4] Arguments about non-sexist language in religious ritual are considerably older than the debate on 'political correctness'; it is only very recently that the term has been invoked by people denouncing feminist interference with language, though the denunciation itself has been going on for 20 years.

Does it make any difference if old issues are talked about in a new language of 'political correctness'? For two reasons, the answer is 'yes, up to a point'. First of all, the fact that the Revd Ducker couched his concerns in the new 'PC' terminology made them instantly newsworthy. Newspapers cashing in on the recent topicality of 'political correctness' have recycled an astonishing amount of hoary old boilerplate about feminist attempts to change the language; much of it could have been (and for all I know was) written in the mid-1970s when the Sex Discrimination Act replaced 'dustmen' with 'refuse collectors' in classified ads across the nation. Secondly, however, the placing of an old issue within the new 'political correctness' frame alters people's perceptions of it. Discursive drift transfers not only the words but also the passions associated with one argument on to other arguments; the implication is that if you don't like campus speech codes or terms like 'physically challenged', you should logically feel the same way about replacing 'mankind' with 'humankind' in prayers. As more and more concerns are gathered under the umbrella of 'political correctness', passions intensify and proposals that were only recently considered innocuous are reinterpreted as sinister emanations of the 'thought police'.

At this point, however, a sceptical reader might well want to ask: are such proposals, however innocuous they may once have seemed, *not* in fact sinister emanations of the thought police? Even if the critics of 'political correctness' have feet of clay, is there not, at the core of their argument, an analysis of the politics of language that we ought to take seriously?

This returns us to the charges against so-called 'political correctness' I mentioned earlier: on one hand that its brand of verbal hygiene abuses language by perverting the meanings of words, and on the other that it trivialises politics by focusing on language and not reality. To these we should add a third accusation, that by telling people what to say – and by implication perhaps even what to think – political correctness poses a threat to free expression. Such arguments raise complex theoretical questions. What is the relation between language and reality? Is there, and could there ever be, a neutral language untainted by any political agenda? In matters of language, how far does our freedom extend?

One thing that must strike anyone considering the above charges is how contradictory they are. How can intervening in language be both a trivial diversion from politics and a threat to our most fundamental liberties? The crudest formulations of the idea that demands for language change are trivial can surely be dismissed as *self*-contradictory. The person who levels this charge does not consider it a trivial matter, or why bother to articulate the objection in the first place? 'If the point is so trivial,' I want to tell this person, 'please humour me by conceding it. If it really doesn't matter whether we write *he* or *s/he* or *she*, then let's just do it my way and both of us will be happy.' Of course, this hypothetical conversation calls attention to a hidden dimension in the dispute, which is not just about the content of linguistic rules but also about who will be permitted to make them for whom.

A related but more thoughtful objection typically comes from liberals rather than conservatives. Barbara Ehrenreich, for instance, in an essay titled 'The challenge for the Left', asserts that changing language changes nothing very much: 'If you outlaw the term "girl" instead of "woman" you're not going to do a thing about the sexist attitudes underneath . . . there is a tendency to confuse verbal purification with real social change . . . Now I'm all for verbal uplift . . . [but] verbal uplift is not the revolution.'[5] In his polemic *Culture of Complaint*, Robert Hughes expresses a similar impatience with 'verbal uplift':

> We want to create a sort of linguistic Lourdes, where evil and misfortune are dispelled by a dip in the waters of euphemism. Does the cripple rise from his wheelchair, or feel better about being stuck in it, because someone . . . decided that, for official purposes, he was 'physically challenged'?[6]

This line of argument begs the question, does anyone actually believe that 'verbal uplift' is, by itself, the revolution? In the 1970s when non-sexist language policies were being developed in many institutions, people who opposed them were fond of saying that modifying pronouns would not get women equal pay. Some of us were equally fond of replying that we never thought it would; but no one was offering a binary choice, *either* equal pay *or* gender-neutral pronouns. Nothing prevented us campaigning for both.

On the other hand, radicals of my generation and succeeding generations do attach more importance to linguistic and other representations than their predecessors did, so that we regard words and images as useful material with which to work for social change. Ours is not only the traditional politics of workplace and neighbourhood organising, but also the mass-media influenced politics of image, spectacle, performance: think of Rock Against Racism, or women dancing on the silos at Greenham Common, or lesbians abseiling into the House of Lords to protest against Clause 28. The same 'turn to culture' can be observed on the radical right: Ellen

Messer-Davidow[7] quotes a US conservative foundation which proclaimed in 1987: 'the politics that carry us into the twenty-first century will be based not on economics, but on culture'. Where the left tries to get on TV, the right tries to buy it; where the left rocks against racism, the right rants against rap or Robert Mapplethorpe. Either way, it is a cultural agenda. No doubt Barbara Ehrenreich is right that cultural politics alone cannot bring about lasting social change, but arguably people who think it 'trivial' have not come to terms with the nature of the societies activists are working to change at the end of the twentieth century.

Ehrenreich and Hughes both raise the question whether changing the words people use by *fiat* does anything to change the way they think. This is certainly an important question, and the scientific jury is still out: most linguists and psychologists today are sceptical about the strong version of the claim that language *determines* perceptions, but on the weaker claim that it can *influence* perceptions there is conflicting evidence.

My own view is that language is a highly variable and radically context-dependent phenomenon which may have effects on perception, but only in conjunction with other factors. For instance, researchers have found in controlled experiments that people do tend to interpret generic masculine terms as referring to men, whereas this tendency is less marked with gender-neutral terms; but even with neutral terminology the tendency to 'think male' is still discernible, and there are many instances of people using neutral terms as if they were masculine (consider George Bush's explanation for the US invasion of Panama: 'We cannot tolerate attacks on the wife of an American citizen'). George Bush's androcentric worldview shows up in his use of language, and drawing attention to that language is an effective way of making a political point about unremarked sexist assumptions; but in this instance the language cannot be said to have *caused* the sexism.

Yet even if we assume that language has no significant effect on perception, that does not license us to dismiss it as a wholly trivial concern; for language is not just about representing private mental states, it is also a public affirmation of values. It seems odd that Barbara Ehrenreich, in a passage that urges us to prefer action over mere words, should place so much emphasis on *attitudes*, arguing that it makes no difference what people say if underneath they are thinking the same old sexist thoughts. Obviously feminists and other radicals would like to change people's attitudes, but from Ehrenreich's own, action-oriented viewpoint, it is surely more important to change their behaviour – which is exactly the intention of a rule prescribing 'woman' rather than 'girl'. How someone treats me publicly matters more than how they feel about me privately; the fact that my boss seethes with inward resentment while addressing me respectfully is less damaging to me than if he addressed me disrespectfully in accordance with his true feelings. (Nina Simone puts the point succinctly in her civil rights anthem 'Mississippi Goddamn': 'you don't have to live next door to me/just give me my equality'.)

There is nothing trivial about trying to institutionalise a public norm of respect rather than disrespect, and one of the most important ways in which respect is made manifest publicly is through linguistic choices: in the context of addressing someone, words are deeds (compare 'Hey, bitch!' with 'Excuse me, Ms Cameron'). As philosopher Trevor Pateman has observed, even the most cynical compliance with anti-sexist norms sets a public example others may take to heart.[8] Changing what counts as acceptable public behaviour is one of the ways you go about changing prevailing attitudes – ask anyone who still smokes.

This brings us to Robert Hughes's scorn for the idea that 'evil and misfortune are dispelled by a dip in the waters of euphemism'. 'Euphemism' has been a keyword in the debate on 'politically correct' language, and it takes its force from one of this century's canonical verbal hygiene texts, George Orwell's 1946 essay 'Politics and the English Language', which is invoked, significantly, by conservatives and liberals alike in defence of the kind of language that 'tells it like it is': plain, clear, concise, unclouded by impenetrable jargon and circumlocution, mind-numbing cliché or emotive, value-laden terms. 'Euphemisms' (like *pass away* for *die*) are disparaged as both circumlocutory and value-laden.

What Orwellians seem to overlook, though, is the difficulty in many cases of finding a neutral term that corresponds to some purported 'euphemism'. Hughes, for instance, appears to be suggesting that whereas *physically challenged* is a ludicrous attempt to gloss over the true condition of the person in the wheelchair, *cripple* would be a perfectly neutral description. I don't know about Hughes, but *cripple* had already been consigned to the realms of playground abuse when I started school 30 years ago.

Another term that has been ridiculed as euphemistic is *African American*. If this is a euphemism, what exactly is it a euphemism *for*? The relationship between *African American* and *Black* (or *colored*, or *Negro*) is only comparable to the relationship between *pass away* and *die* if you make an assumption I suspect few liberals would want to admit to. If, for the sake of argument, we take the charge of euphemism seriously, and ask what is being 'covered up' in using *African American* instead of *Black*, *colored* or *Negro*, the only answer that comes to mind is the skin colour of the people in question. If so, is that not precisely the point of the linguistic intervention – to challenge the kind of discourse that defines people by skin colour? Someone who claims *African American* is a euphemism because it makes no reference to skin colour is implicitly asserting that a description of people by skin colour is a value-neutral description.

The kind of verbal hygiene characterised as 'PC' rejects the simple Orwellian opposition between neutral terms and loaded ones, drawing attention to the fact that *all* words come with values attached, and moreover that these are variable depending on who is speaking, in what context and within what structure of power. (For example, 'nigger' and 'queer' obviously have a different value used by an East End skinhead and by the performers Niggas With Attitude, or the activists of Queer Nation.) The idea that any terms – let alone terms like *cripple* and *Black* – just neutrally denote their referents, that their meanings are the same for every speaker in every context, and that they do not change over time, presupposes an extraordinarily naïve account of the way language works, as though it were a giant codebook placing words in a fixed one-to-one correspondence with meanings, which must then be defended to the death on pain of forfeiting all ability to communicate.

As I tried to show by analysing the history of the term 'politically correct', words are constantly being inflected and reinflected with new meanings as they are used in different contexts and media, carried over into new spheres of discourse and deployed in arguments among people with conflicting beliefs and interests. This potential for reinflection is exactly what both the 'politically correct' and their right-wing opponents are exploiting: deliberately, strategically, and very much 'in your face'.

In a universe of communications like the one present-day English speakers inhabit, no single constituency can control the meaning-making process, and even where communications are less diffuse it is not in the nature of meaning to be fixed (for this reason, Orwell's Newspeak, the instrument of the thought police, strikes the linguist as a singularly unconvincing creation). At the same time, some people and institutions (those which codify and regulate public usage, including the mass media) have more influence than others in determining which meanings will have the widest circulation and credibility in a given time and place. It would be misguided simply to reverse the terms of the argument by calling this 'thought policing', but it is certainly a form of gatekeeping whose implications we do well to ponder. It is always worth asking why, and from whose point of view, one way of using language seems obvious, natural and neutral, while another seems ludicrous, loaded and perverse.

This, in fact, is the central question the so-called 'politically correct' have posed about language. It is in their answer to it that we will find the real reason for the alarm with which so many liberals as well as conservatives have greeted their proposals. If the radical account of language is right, it challenges fundamental liberal assumptions about both language and society.

*

Considered in its totality, the debate on 'political correctness' is most obviously a debate about how democracies made up of diverse populations subscribing to a variety of beliefs and customs are to preserve a common culture. The conservative answer to that question prescribes the assimilation of subordinated groups – take it or leave it, play by our rules or quit the field. The liberal answer by contrast makes much of the idea that differing opinions can be exchanged and debated in a public sphere of free and rational discourse, to produce, if not consensus, then at least a civil compromise.

Central to this liberal ideal is the notion that people speaking from widely divergent standpoints can nevertheless find a common language in which to talk to one another. The language that is assumed to serve this purpose best is more or less the kind Orwell championed: a plain and transparent language that gets to the essence of things without passing judgement upon them and thereby predetermining the outcome of the exchange or reducing it to an uncivil shouting match.

Some forms of verbal hygiene that are now placed under the heading of 'political correctness' were acceptable to many liberals at the time they were proposed because they seemed to be in line with this model of language as ideally the 'mirror of nature'. For example, feminists campaigning for non-sexist language often used the argument that such language was more accurate, more true to reality, than the traditional masculine alternative. After all, they said, there are women as well as men in the world, and today those women are more visible than ever before. Shouldn't our language reflect this reality? They also placed emphasis on civility, the simple virtue of not giving needless offence – another aim liberals could wholeheartedly support.

Now, though, it has become clearer that some verbal hygienists are grounding their claims in a very different kind of argument: far from trying to contribute to a common language that faithfully represents reality and respects the sensitivities of everyone, they are denying that any such language exists, or ever has existed, or ever could. They are suggesting that the illusion of a common language depends on making everyone accept definitions which may be presented as neutral and universal, but which in fact represent the particular standpoint of straight white men from the most privileged social classes. They are asking why they can only get into the conversation on terms set by that small elite; and by proposing to set their own terms, they are deliberately destabilising what had been taken as an unproblematic and neutral means of communication.

Despite the apocalyptic claims of the anti-PC lobby, empirical investigation suggests that linguistic militants have not succeeded in imposing their terms on everyone. What they have brilliantly succeeded in doing, though, is in some ways even more threatening. Meaning works by contrast: the words you choose acquire force from an implicit comparison with the ones you could have chosen, but did not. By coining alternatives to traditional usage, therefore, the radicals have effectively *politicised all the terms*. They have made it impossible for anyone to speak or write without appearing to take up a political position, for which they can then be held accountable. Thus if I say, 'Ms X is the chair of Y' I convey one political standpoint; if I say 'Miss X is the chairman of Y' I convey another. What I cannot do any more is say either of these things and hope to convey by it only 'a certain woman holds a certain office in a certain organisation'.

It is this politicising of people's words against their will, rather than specific usages like 'African American' or 'physically challenged', that I believe many critics find so deeply objectionable. They are genuinely bewildered that women or members of minority groups should persist in reading bizarre connotations into perfectly innocent words whose meanings should surely be transparent to anyone, since they are simply facts of the language. To which the women, etc., are likely to retort: 'On the contrary, they are *arte*facts of your historical power to define words for everyone.'

There is no doubt this is a radical challenge to a tradition that has made the stable and consensual order of language into a metaphor for other kinds of stability, consensus and order – social, moral and political. But just as the stability and orderliness of language has been overestimated, so the threat posed to civil discourse by the partial breakdown of that order is being wildly exaggerated.

As Stanley Fish points out in his provocatively entitled book *There's No Such Thing as Speech: and it's a good thing too*!,[9] language has no meaning in the absence of rules and restrictions that make some ways of talking unacceptable, or just unintelligible. Since speech free from *all* constraints would be inconsequential gibberish, 'freedom of speech' can only mean 'freedom within certain limits'. But those limits may be set in such a way that dominant groups do not notice them. They talk of free speech as an absolute, even as they deny the legitimacy of other people's ways of speaking. As the others rise up in protest, the norms that govern public discourse are subject to contestation and revision – a process that has always figured in political struggle.

The *New York Magazine* article that led my friend to throw away her T-shirt warned that 'making people watch what they say is the central preoccupation of politically correct students'. I find myself wondering why this – not even telling people *what* to say, but making them *watchful* about it – should be presented as such a self-evidently terrible thing. If we care about language (and critics of 'PC' are pre-eminent among those who profess to care about it very deeply), why on earth should we not pay close attention to the implications of what comes out of our mouths?

The verbal hygiene movement for so-called 'politically correct' language does not threaten our freedom to speak as we choose, within the limits imposed by any form of social and public interaction. It threatens only our freedom to imagine that our linguistic choices are inconsequential, or to suppose that any one group of people has an inalienable right to prescribe them.

NOTES

1 21 January 1991.
2 'A Short History of the Term *Politically Correct*', *Beyond PC: Toward A Politics of Understanding*, P. Aufderheide (ed.), Graywolf Press, 1992.
3 'Political Correctness and Identity Politics', (*Beyond PC: Toward A Politics of Understanding*, P Aufderheide (ed.), Graywolf Press, 1992.
4 *Guardian*, 30 June 1992.
5 'The Challenge for the Left', *Debating PC: The Controversy Over Political Correctness on College Campuses*, P. Berman (ed.), USA, Laurel, 1992.

6 OUP, 1993.
7 'Manufacturing the attack on liberalised Higher Education', *Social Text* 36, 1993.
8 *Language, Truth and Politics*, Lewes: Jean Stroud, 1980.
9 OUP, 1994.

I would like to thank the following for their assistance with this essay: Meryl Altman, Mary Dearborn, Bill Defotis, Lucinda DeWitt, Simon Frith and Keith Nightenhelser.

Melanie Phillips

ILLIBERAL LIBERALISM

A few years ago, something very strange happened. People started to reproach me for becoming reactionary and right-wing. Since I came from a liberal, left-of-centre background and had worked for most of my professional life for the *Guardian* newspaper, this was a disconcerting experience. One minute the government was criticising my allegedly left-wing views towards the poor, or sick, or jobless, or immigrants; the next I was being condemned by people on the left for being a traitor to the cause.

Was it true? I inspected myself anxiously for evidence of a change of political personality. I seemed to be still concerned about justice and liberty and official lies and the fate of the most vulnerable and dispossessed. Yet I was increasingly finding myself out of step with colleagues, friends and a number of readers. Was I simply following in the footsteps of all those writers and thinkers who had moved from left to right as age had withered them? Was I, like a piece of litmus paper dipped into the surrounding culture, changing from pink to blue?

It would be idle to pretend one does not change with age. Having children, in particular, tends to have a profound and salutary effect upon one's perspectives. But if I have changed, I believe it is because something pretty profound has happened to the liberal culture that formed the bedrock of my beliefs. To my growing perplexity, a creed that for me was supposed to embody tolerance has come to represent intolerance. Purporting to help the oppressed, it has itself become an instrument of oppression. Views that offend against this new orthodoxy are suppressed through professional and social ostracism that plays upon the deeply rooted fear of the liberal intelligentsia that they might be thought to be illiberal. The anxiety not to be thought judgemental has turned into a denial of any judgement at all, for fear of causing offence or denying people their rights. Even language has been rewritten and certain words banned from use, amounting to censorship in the name of individual rights.

It has been all the more bewildering because these developments were rooted in values and thought processes that I myself had shared. Political correctness may have appeared to be a phenomenon that sprang up on American campuses in the late 1980s. But its ideological ancestry lay in the social and intellectual revolution of the 1960s, which had no less profound an effect on Britain. That revolution rejected the authoritarian rules of social intercourse that previously placed unacceptable limits on liberty and human rights. I grew to adulthood during this time, and formed a strong and lasting identification with social justice and individual rights. The great movement for women's emancipation, the determination to sweep away prejudice against ethnic or sexual minorities or disabled people, the wariness of authority and consequent promotion of intellectual dissent and nonconformity, these were the banners behind which I marched. I believed all these causes to be noble, and still do. Fighting injustice flows naturally from my own Jewish culture, which bears the ineradicable imprint of oppression and prejudice.

But then, in the 1980s, it seemed to me that those very ideals began to stand on their heads. And in my view it was no accident that this strange inversion coincided with the arrival of a particularly authoritarian and long-lasting Conservative government. Mrs Thatcher remade the whole machinery of government in her image. Anyone who was not 'one of us' was cast into the wilderness of political opposition. As the years rolled on with no change of government in sight, an alternative establishment grew up of those on the left who had been excluded from any power over public life. And so it seemed to me that instead of operating in the public sphere, the left were forced to exercise their power in the one area still open to them – the private sphere of personal behaviour.

The result was a remarkable mirror image of political conformity. The Conservative government, committed to an individualistic free-for-all in economics, represented nevertheless an anti-intellectual conformity rooted in prejudice and ignorance. Any groups who threatened this conformity were to be ostracised. So immigrants were to be feared, those without jobs despised and the poor written out of the script altogether. I find this intolerable. But I also think that the opponents of Conservatism have been trapped into a parallel conformity.

For the belief took hold on that side of the argument that we were all in some way guilty of oppression. Now, it seems to me to be a truism that we all harbour prejudices, just as we are all prone to selfishness, or jealousy, or any number of characteristics that make up every human being. But understanding the latent prejudices in human nature appeared to develop into the belief that everyone in majority groups exercised those prejudices, and that society was endemically oppressive as a result. The result seemed to me to be that, in some cases, people whose behaviour was blameless were attacked for behaving in a prejudiced manner, simply because they were part of the majority.

Meanwhile, the 'victim' class was infantilised by having its own human flaws or weaknesses denied. The result was not only injustice, but also that people whose interests I cared about – ethnic minorities, poor or ill-educated people – were ironically made into double victims. They were trapped between real prejudice and bigotry on one side and patronising and false assumptions on the other. This seemed to me to be a most unholy alliance. It also represented a betrayal by the left which wasn't really surprising. The left, after all, claims monopoly rights on virtue. Yet history teaches us that self-appointed moral guardians who believe theirs is the only true faith all too often turn into oppressors. That lesson, I believe, has now repeated itself.

It was in the mid-1980s that I first began to find I was losing my political bearings in a topsy-turvy universe where facts meant whatever the upholders of social virtue wanted them to mean. I was strongly opposed to market forces and the whole minimalist state project, as indeed I remain. Yet I began to become uncomfortably aware that Tory newspapers were saying certain things I realised were true – and which were being denied at the liberal end of the market. In particular, they were making some devastating criticisms of the education system. The charge was that teachers were failing to teach children properly; that emphasis on literacy and numeracy was being replaced by a child-centred philosophy that devalued rules and was inimical to the imparting of knowledge; and that the children who were suffering most were those from disadvantaged backgrounds for whom schools were the one lifeline out of the ghettos of poverty.

The conventional wisdom on the left was that this was politically motivated malice. The 'truth' was apparently that education was being run down by a government determined to starve schools of adequate resources and denigrate the teaching profession. In fact, the position was more complicated. It was true that the government was denigrating the teachers. But from where I was sitting, it seemed that they could hardly complain since they appeared constantly to devalue their own skills and seemed not to understand the disciplines a true profession imposed.

However, such complexities were not acknowledged by people who saw nothing wrong with the education system except for government antagonism. Such people were mainly complacent, well-to-do, white middle-class folk who made social capital out of sending their children to state schools but who were happy to play the system by moving house into the catchment area of the best (i.e. middle-class) establishments, or paying for private tutors. They often came from the kind of backgrounds which meant they simply had no imaginative grasp of the importance of school to a child living in social and intellectual poverty. The idea of a ladder up meant nothing to people who, to my mind at least, made a virtue out of talking down. Because, after all, they felt they knew best. They *knew*, for instance, that teaching children to read by tried and tested reading schemes was wrong, because it gave slower children a feeling of failure, just as they also *knew* that teaching children historical facts or mathematical formulae was wrong because it denied the higher truths of subjective creativity.

Descended as I am from poor Jewish immigrants, coming from a culture that understood from painful experience that education was the only pathway into the social mainstream, I believed that this was itself elitist prejudice, displayed by individuals whose belief in their own monopoly of wisdom was not only patronising but deeply damaging to the very people they claimed to champion. As far back as the late 1970s, when the then Labour Prime Minister James Callaghan was so worried about standards that he introduced the Great Debate on education, comparative education statistics showed that the UK was producing relatively ill-educated school-leavers who were unable to compete in world markets. The social casualties, the young people who had no jobs or who were involved in crime, had more often than not been failed lamentably by the education system. HM

Inspectors of Education constantly repeated warnings that teachers were undervaluing their pupils. Yet how could it be that the lying, unscrupulous Tory press was getting this right while the caring, responsible, liberal press was pretending it wasn't happening? It seemed to me that liberal journalists were so frightened of being labelled right-wing that they simply closed their eyes to the reality.

I recall vividly an encounter with a young West Indian community worker in Tottenham, angrily denouncing the ideology that had given young Black people like himself an inferior education, denying them the teaching that could have equipped them to compete, refusing to give them the knowledge they needed of maths and language and history, all in the name of some white middle-class fantasy of equality that was actually going to keep them trapped in disadvantage. 'They teach them all these things in private schools,' he said; 'that's why those children go on to run everything. So why aren't they teaching them to us?' His anger wasn't directed at Mrs Thatcher's government. Unlike white liberals, whom he despised, he didn't want his council to have more money to spend on schools. Instead, he said he wanted West Indian children to be helped to be educated in private schools, and he railed bitterly against the Labour council for blocking the planning permission to enable this to happen. He had understood that Black youngsters like himself had been cheated by a liberal culture on a guilt trip. To me, this wasn't liberalism at all. This was anti-liberalism. It was freedom betrayed.

When I started to explore some of this in my column in the *Guardian*, the full fury of the liberal establishment was unleashed. One particular article I wrote questioned the educationally correct opinion that there was no correct way to write or speak English. It seems to me that full command of the language is an essential precondition for people to gain control over their own lives. The politically correct view, however, was that Standard English was elitist and individual patois just as valid. Indeed, an official report in 1988 on the teaching of English to primary schoolchildren genuflected to this orthodoxy by saying that Standard English should be taught only because it had 'social prestige' but that it was nevertheless merely 'a technical term' for a dialect with particular uses and should not be confused with 'proper, good or correct English'. Proper, good and correct were, in the new orthodoxy, such value-laden terms they could no longer be acknowledged to hold any value whatsoever. Yet depriving ethnic minority children of a mastery of Standard English would inevitably disadvantage them in a society run by people who took its benefits for granted, only to deny them to others.

For me, a cultural relativism had taken over. But when I said that I received dozens of furious letters from lecturers in education outraged at the suggestion that their philosophy of teaching was having any adverse effects on schoolchildren. Dr Barry Stierer, for instance, lecturer in education at the Open University, wrote of his satisfaction that children were performing badly in 'traditional' reading tests since this showed the 'success of the nation's teachers, who were increasingly inviting young children to approach reading from the beginning as a meaningful and enjoyable activity'. On the contrary, this celebration of failure, supported by the false antithesis between 'meaningful and enjoyable' and success at learning to read, seemed to me to demonstrate a most alarming and arrogant disregard for the right of every child to master the language.

I got into even more trouble when I spoke out in favour of a retired headmaster, John Sanders, who had written in the *Guardian* that teachers were deliberately marginalising themselves. Their role as expert, guide, leader and trainer, he wrote, had given way to the passive role of 'facilitator', leaving children to find things out for themselves. The result, he suggested, was meaningless work, bored and misbehaving children, harassed teachers and under-achievement. My support for Mr Sanders produced a bulging and memorable postbag, in which I was denounced variously as 'ignorant, silly, intellectually vulgar, vicious, irresponsible, elitist, middle-class, fatuous, dangerous, intemperate, shallow, strident, reactionary, near-hysterical, propagandist, simplistic, well-paid, unbalanced, prejudiced, rabid, venomous, pathetic'.

It was hard to say which shocked me more – the intemperate and abusive nature of such educationists' reactions, or their justification of what seemed to me to be a betrayal of the right of children to be educated. What on earth had happened to those ideals of the 1960s? Was this really what the pursuit of equality had come down to, a vicious downward spiral of under-achievement promulgated by professionals paying lip-service to a politically correct goal?

I was not alone in thinking that, far from liberals devoted to tolerance, there was an intellectual lynch mob out there. Defenders of the new orthodoxy liked to caricature all their opponents as the loony right, but this simply wasn't true. In 1987, the four-strong history department at Lewes Priory comprehensive school in East Sussex decided that the GCSE exam was preventing them from teaching history properly. The new history, they felt, devalued facts and substituted peripheral concepts such as cause and effect or evidence skills. Three of them – the department head Chris McGovern, his deputy Anthony Freeman and Arthur Franklin – offered their pupils an alternative syllabus, the Scottish O grade, which they felt was a more appropriate history exam. The result was that the three lost their jobs. Mr Franklin, who had a master's degree, was eventually re-employed in a tertiary college, but Mr McGovern, who had a first-class degree in history, and Dr Freeman, who had a PhD, were retrained as a primary school teacher and an adviser on school trips and blackballed from teaching in secondary schools.

Teachers and other educationists who wrote to me provided more evidence that the new liberalism was anything but. Again, these weren't new right activists, but ordinary teachers up and down the country who were appalled at what was happening. They wrote clandestinely, with baroque accounts of how they had to conceal their ordered and successful teaching methods whenever the education inspectors came round, forced to rearrange their classrooms in fashionable and unproductive disorder for fear of losing their prospects of promotion or even their jobs. One education psychologist wrote in 1990: 'In my job I see small children whose listening skills and ability to stay focused on a task are chronic. Yet they are put to learn in an environment which no undergraduate would have to suffer . . . Children do not learn through play, but through instruction, explanation, guidance, motivation from an adult . . . and whenever I say this to a group of teachers, the older and wiser members of the group come to me afterwards and thank me for saying it, they have been waiting for years for someone to make this point. But for some reason they cannot say this in public. And neither can I; which is why I do not want my name published. My job is important to me and public condemnation of teaching methods will not be approved.'

To me, such evidence revealed a startling abuse of power, more reminiscent of the intellectual intimidation practised by totalitarian regimes. And in a strange way, it also mirrored the bullying practised by the Conservative government, which threatened employees in the health service with dismissal, for example, if they blew the whistle on the failure of the government's market ideology. Intimidation on the right was being matched by intimidation on the left. Both sides were in the business of enforcing conformity, although to very different standards.

Behind these battles in the classroom lay the new certainties of educational theory, which seemed to have junked traditional liberal ideals of education in favour of a wholly subjective intention to redress a perceived set of cultural imbalances. One English literature don, a woman in her thirties, reflected to me privately on the fact that for the past 20 years, English faculties had been preoccupied with ridding the canon of English literature of dead, white, male authors. She herself had been an enthusiastic soldier in this crusade. Now, though, she was horrified. Her students were ignorant, ill-educated, grossly underread. They found it hard to see any difference in value between good and bad writers because they had been taught that value itself was a worthless concept. Yet she would never say this in public because it would be tantamount to professional suicide. Like many others, she asked to remain anonymous.

The project, then, was nothing less than to correct the

value system of English literature. To that end, a range of children's books fell foul of the ideological censors. I read about and heard of discussions by librarians and teachers about the texts they refused to stock or teach on the grounds that they might poison young minds. Yet one of the defining motifs of the cultural revolution of the 1960s was freedom of expression and the rejection of censorship as authoritarian. For liberals, there was a particular irony in the traditions behind the new voluntary censorship. In the early nineteenth century, Dr Bowdler and his sister started to expurgate Shakespeare, a movement which led to the progressive doctoring of a range of works – novels by Fielding, Sterne, Smollett, Swift, the Victorian novelists, the Bible. Traditional bowdlerism targeted sexual explicitness and profanity. Modern bowdlerites train their sights on race, ethnicity, class and gender. Both represent an attempt to stamp out evil by people who claim to be the arbiters of goodness; the definition of evil has merely shifted with the century.

As Noel Perrin writes in *Dr Bowdler's Legacy*,[1] while sexual prudery diminished ethnic prudery increased. We may now reveal *Gulliver's Travels* and *The Canterbury Tales* in their entirety, but, Perrin says, *Charlie and the Chocolate Factory* and *Mary Poppins* have now been bowdlerised in the United States, Walter de la Mare and Kipling in Britain. Most famously, he cites *Dr Doolittle* as expurgated in both countries. The once dark-skinned Prince Bumpo survives, neither Black nor white but colourless, which changes the plot. Yet this neo-bowdlerism is selective. If similar attempts were made to rid literature of its anti-semitism, there would be very large gaps indeed. T. S. Eliot's 'The rats are underneath the piles / The Jew is underneath the lot', survives unmarked by opprobrium. In this brave new value system, being beastly to Jews apparently passes the test of political correctness. Once again the self-styled arbiters of goodness turn out to embody partial and highly questionable judgements, in the name of which they seek to deny to others the opportunity to exercise their own.

It seems to me that the main purpose of today's bowdlerism is less to protect the ostensible targets of prejudice – Black people, women or whomever – than to demonstrate the moral purity of the expurgators, their sensitivity to the evils of prejudice and discrimination. This cult of sensibility, which in pre-Victorian times had become synonymous with recognising the difference between good and evil, goes right back to the writings of the philosopher Rousseau; and it is Rousseau who holds the key to the paradox of political correctness, the illiberal face of liberalism. Rousseau was an anti-liberal, whose professed belief in liberty threaded through Robespierre to Hitler. Yet his Romantic ideas grew out of liberalism. Early liberalism stood for religious toleration, respect for the rights of property and the belief that all men were born equal. Rousseau extended liberal individualism from the intellect to the emotions. His *Social Contract* of 1762 was supposed to enshrine principles of freedom but in fact called up the spectre of a totalitarian state. To protect individual freedom, he wrote, every individual had to give up all his rights to the whole community. The general will ruled and anyone who refused to obey would be forced to do so. Since the general will was supposed to protect liberty, this doctrine meant nothing less than that people were forced to be free.

Forcing people to be free, it seems to me, lurks at the very heart of modern political correctness. It drives the projects to make us all confess our racism or deny that there are norms of behaviour. It is creating tyrannies of intellectual coercion particularly in academic institutions, whose traditions of liberal tolerance make them vulnerable to charges of bigotry. And just as Rousseau's pursuit of freedom created the opposite result, so these politically correct attitudes help bring about the very prejudices they purport to despise.

In the public sector, the drive to eradicate racism, for example, has created pockets of oppressiveness which are not only unjust but also increase racism and disadvantage Black and other vulnerable people. Take the thorny arena of social work. Directors of council social services departments say they feel helpless to tackle the inadequacies of Black staff because they know that to challenge them is likely to produce allegations of a racial witchhunt. The result is that vulnerable clients, some of whom will be Black themselves, are ill-served by inadequate staff. Anti-racism, which started out with the worthy intention of righting a wrong, has developed into a zealotry which creates instead fresh victims. This anti-liberal mind-twist now passes for orthodoxy in many social science departments.

In the 1980s, the social workers' training body, the Central Council for Education and Training in Social Work (CCETSW), began to embody this philosophy in its directives for social work training. If universities refused to comply with them, the accreditation of their social work training courses would be put at risk. These directives required such courses to teach that 'racism is endemic in the values, attitudes and structures of British society, including those of social services and social work education', and that 'steps need to be taken to promote permeation of all aspects of the curriculum by an anti-racist analysis'. These attitudes were not based on liberal notions. On the contrary, they specifically rejected them. One CCETSW training pack produced in 1993, *Antiracist Social Work Education*, says:

> Social work values are based on liberal ideas about freedom, tolerance, individualism, and are presented to us as separate from political realities – they are seen as universal, separate, sacred. They result in such beliefs as:
>
> - every point of view is equal to every other;
> - you have to win people over by rational persuasion, not emotional arguments;
> - you must not interfere with other people's freedom of speech/action (even if it is racist/sexist);
> - eventually everyone will oppose racism when they've heard all the arguments.
>
> Although we all know that this way of working is not an effective way of achieving change, and is indeed guaranteed to maintain the status quo, it is still presented to us as the best possible method of going about things . . . Anti-racist practice requires the adoption of explicit values which identify with oppressed groups, which see individual problems as having roots in political structures, not in individual or cultural pathology.

Now of course, racial prejudice and discrimination are evils that we should guard against and fight. But the anti-racism taught to trainee social workers has nothing to do with promoting freedom and equality. These paragraphs

I have quoted explicitly throw out tolerance and individualism. The CCETSW emphasis on anti-racism is predicated on the belief that racism is all-pervading. Universities are instructed to teach this without needing to produce the evidence to back up this comprehensive claim. At a stroke, traditional liberal ideas about intellectual inquiry being based on the rules of evidence are junked. And of course such evidence does not exist. We do know that certain institutions have racist cultures, and that racial prejudice is a general problem. But it does not follow from that that *all* institutions behave in a prejudiced manner. Such an assertion is little better than propaganda.

It also follows, of course, that if racism is 'endemic' in every British institution, then every individual associated with them is suspect until proved otherwise. To me, this is the recipe for a witchhunt. And indeed, I discovered to my horror that this was indeed the case. From my inquiries around a number of universities and social services departments, and from conversations I had with traumatised ex-social workers – all of whom conformed to liberal, Labour Party-leaning profiles – I discovered that unless staff and students on social work courses 'confessed' to their own racism, they would be pressurised until they did so. Staff were reduced to tears when told that their refusal to confess to racism was proof that they were racist. 'Monitoring groups' were expected to sit in on these sessions to ensure the correct line was pursued. Many adverse consequences followed. Tutors told me that some of the better students got out altogether. But what particularly worried the tutors and social services directors was that so much time was spent on anti-racism training, the social workers ended up inadequately trained to meet the far more pressing needs of their clients. Occasional inklings of what was going on filtered out to the public, such as when a mixed race couple were prevented from adopting a Black child in 1993 because the Asian would-be adoptive mother said she had never experienced racism. In the surrealist world of political correctness, it is of course deemed impossible for a Black person *not* to encounter racism. So that person's actual experience must be denied.

Family values, and in particular the rise in the number of single parents, have become another highly contentious issue. It has become extremely difficult to say in liberal circles that children are by and large best served when they are brought up by both their natural parents. This is despite an overwhelming body of evidence, both from social scientists and professionals working with children, that this is the case. But to say so invites professional or political marginalisation and rejection. This is because people are anxious above all else not to give offence to parents who may be divorced or who never married. This powerful imperative, to give no offence, means that no one behaviour can be held to be superior to any other. Yet this particular expression of individualism unfortunately produces social casualties – the children. So inconvenient is this fact to the prevailing orthodoxy that the evidence supporting it is ignored, misrepresented or denied and those who bear witness to it are insulted and condemned in an attempt to shut them up.

When I started writing about family values, I was astonished by what I felt was a widespread intellectual dishonesty on one side of the argument. It seemed to me that both the literature and the childcare professionals I talked to presented an overwhelming case that fractured families caused lasting pain, distress and damage to the children involved. There appeared to be a continuum of child misery, stretching from rowing parents, through separation and divorce all the way to the arrival of step-parents, in many cases a disaster for the still-grieving children. Yet many social scientists appeared to disregard this evidence, promoting instead the idea that it was better for the children if unhappy parents split up. In certain extreme cases – if there was violence, for example – this was obviously so; but the majority of fractured families were not in such extreme positions.

The eminent sociologist Professor A. H. Halsey staunchly declared these facts, only to be dismissed with rage and contempt by other academics who told me he had 'gone ga-ga'. I had a remarkable telephone conversation with one such academic, who had said Halsey had got it wrong. After I had pressed him repeatedly to tell me what the evidence was to prove Halsey wrong, he finally admitted that Halsey was actually right on the facts. But then he added, by way of explanation: 'What do these people want? Do they want unhappy parents to stay together?' It was all very well to talk about the rights of the children, he expostulated, but what about the rights of the parents?

It seemed to me that this got to the heart of the matter. The analysis could not be admitted because of the fear of the consequences. In this clash between the rights of children and their parents, the adult world had won simply by denying that the price of their freedom was their children's best interests. I thought this was an unforgivable betrayal of vulnerable children. But when I started to write about these matters, I discovered to my distress that I too was now a target for condemnation and misrepresentation. What I had written turned up in distorted form in other critical articles in the press. I was referred to as a 'moraliser', which appeared to be a term of abuse. I was told to my face by erstwhile friends that I had become a reactionary fellow-traveller of the right. 'Don't you realise,' exclaimed one such furious 'friend' virtually as soon as I had walked through the door at some social gathering, 'that it is the *nuclear* family that produces dysfunctional children?'

It seemed to me that this was an issue where the personal and the political had become fatally enmeshed. Ostensible debates about policy were nothing of the kind. Empirical evidence was simply being wrenched out of shape by the self-justification of the divorced/separated/single parent/step-parent status of the protagonists of value-free family relationships. Just as with education or race, what had started out as an affirmation of individual rights had produced adverse consequences because certain bedrock principles had somehow been lost sight of along the way. And if we manage to look at these issues as calmly and as fairly as we can, it seems to me that they pose urgent and difficult questions about the kind of society we want to live in.

As I have noted earlier, we are living through an era of ironic political parallels. The Conservative government has pursued a policy of economic, libertarian individualism which it has applied coercively. Its leftist critics follow a creed of social, egalitarian individualism which they too apply coercively. Both purport to celebrate freedom but effectively deny it. Both are disastrous news for community and the common good. They raise urgent questions about the limitations of liberalism in producing a fair, tolerant and well-ordered society. Supporters of communitarian ethics, which relate behaviour to its impact upon society, suggest that individual rights must be reconsidered in the context of the common good, a corrective and restraining influence that liberals denounce for being authoritarian. But as the American professor of government Michael Sandel argues,[2] intolerance actually flourishes where life is dislocated, roots unsettled and traditions undone. The modern, totalitarian impulse, he writes, springs less from the conviction of confidently situated selves than from the confusions of atomised, dislocated, frustrated selves.

We live in atomised, dislocated and frustrating times. The intolerant paradoxes of political correctness spring directly from those cultural confusions. Our response must surely be to fight intolerance under whatever banner it marches, and to assert instead intellectual freedom and moral integrity. But we should do so with humility and an open mind, lest we fall victim to the very same intellectual hubris that now so fetters our freedom of thought and expression.

NOTES

1 David Godine, 1992.
2 *Liberalism and its Critics*, Blackwell, 1984.

Yasmin Alibhai-Brown

THE GREAT BACKLASH

When I arrived in this country 22 years ago as a refugee, my joy was boundless. Beyond the usual delusions about the motherland, I felt I was leaving behind a cultural outback to live in the heart of greatness. The loss of my home, my country, my friends meant little then. I had spent three years previously at Makerere University in Uganda in the English department where white and Black academics had been transforming the curriculum. They wanted it not only to encapsulate the great Western classics because that was the bedrock of good literature but also to begin to embrace the pulsating new writing that was emerging from those whose voices had been stifled by the experience of slavery and colonialism. Not only did I, therefore, have the opportunity to gorge on the usual venerated texts, but I read Camara Laye, Okot P. Bitek, Chinua Achebe, Michael Antony, Okello Uculi, James Ngugi – as he was then – Leopold Senghor, Sembene Ousmane, Mongo Beti, James Baldwin, Richard Wright, Frantz Fanon, Eldridge Cleaver, V. S. Naipaul and Edgar Mittelholzer whose wonderful book *Corentyne Thunder*, about Guyanese peasant life, still haunts me. I remember wondering why a man like him who had managed after so many struggles to get published in *England* should then choose to kill himself there as he did in 1958.

Overwhelmed, in every sense of the word, after my arrival here, I entered the unreal world of Oxford as a postgraduate student. During my interview, when I was enthusing about V. S. Naipaul, one supercilious lecturer, who did not recognise the name, drawled: 'Well, perhaps you'd be better off going to Leeds or somewhere like that if you are interested in that sort of thing.' 'No no, that is what I *used* to be interested in,' I responded quickly, thinking, I'll just settle myself here amongst Wordsworth and George Eliot, in my Laura Ashley frocks, and you won't know the difference between me and the next Eng. Lit. girl. Looking back, it was the first revelation to me of how closed, restricted and limiting intellectual life became when it turned defensive and obsessive about the preservation of what was undoubtedly great and closed its doors to anything that was new and entirely different. I was better educated than many of my peers at Oxford because I had had this extraordinary exposure to world literature. They thought they were better educated than me because they hadn't. In spite of the pride I felt in having had this tri-cultural background, I never had the audacity to challenge them.

I do now. And so do a great many others. The opening up of the academic canon is just one of the ways in which I and others like me have moved from being supplicants to demanding a greater equality. So for me, what is contemptuously called political correctness is not an intellectual aberration that has burst upon us, but part of a long ideological and political struggle that goes back to the abolition of slavery and decolonisation and is connected to the rise of feminism, anti-racism and multiculturalism. The backlash comes at a time when PC is beginning to get serious. This is perhaps not surprising. While in the past liberals who had and have the power to make you matter even to your own people, encouraged a modicum of rebellion which gave them a wonderful frisson that they were being open, receptive and even bold, what they couldn't tolerate was a real shake-up of the power relationship. Which is just what PC set out to do. As a result there is now a massive defence of the status quo which in part distracts from the continuing realities of racial, cultural, gender and other inequalities. The attack on PC is a kind of back to basics campaign. And the most dispiriting aspect of it is how many liberals have joined in. If you want evidence, a casual count of articles on PC over the past three years shows over 250 attacks, many by liberals, and just a handful of attempts to redress the balance.

We can only understand what has been happening with the onslaught on PC through a critical study of some of these articles and an understanding of the recent political, social and economic changes that have been taking place in the West today. What we now call PC is not new. Back in the 1960s, it was accepted by most thinking people that we needed to get rid of words like 'nigger', 'coon' and 'yid' because language had a bearing on societal attitudes. Then as now, fighting for the word was a symbolic act which represented a fight for a different, fairer world. In Britain, the 1960s, 1970s and early 1980s saw slow but genuine developments in equality legislation and multicultural education. Highly respectable people in this country like Anthony Rampton, Professor Eggleston, Lord Swann – all impeccably middle-class worthies – backed this because they were convinced that white and Black children needed an education that would liberate them from the ideas that might once have been appropriate to a homogeneous imperial country. The disturbances in Brixton led to other luminaries like Lord Scarman taking up the cause of equal rights.

The rise of individualism, monetarism, the new right in Britain, and also the fact that many of these equality initiatives were actually making an impact, inevitably led to attacks on policies engaged in corrective measures. The right-wing press working with politicians started reconstructing myths of past glories, in order to create political unity out of a notion of an inherited *common* white civilisation. This, for example, is what Margaret Thatcher said in a keynote speech on Europe in Bruges in 1990: 'surely what strikes us most is our common experience. For instance, the story of how Europeans explored and colonised and yes, without apology – civilised much of the world.' This beatific vision of what Europe was and could be necessarily excluded sixteen million non-white Europeans who exist merely to service the grand project. It has to be acknowledged that those on the right knew what they wanted and found the most strategic way of getting it. Public opinion was swayed by stories like those about 'loony' councils banning black bin-liners because they were offensive to Blacks or sending spies into schools to weed out racists – most of which were later proved to be false – or examples of unfair preferential treatment. Policies which claimed to be dealing with these insanities won the Conservatives massive support. As society got more and more fragmented this was a useful uniting force. The revisionists had won the day. Multiculturalism and anti-racism were wiped off the agenda. How did they do it?

Firstly by creating a peril out of the flimsiest of evidence, just as with PC now. Even in America, PC is neither the masticating, all-powerful machine nor the mad conspiracy it has been made out to be. Yes there were a few fanatics who wanted to trash all things white/male/heterosexual/middle class and who advocated an inverted kind of racial hatred – afrocentrist academics like Leonard Jeffries who used to head the Black Studies department at City University, New York, simply substituted white supremacy for equally abhorrent 'theories' about Black supremacy and anti-semitic propaganda. And there were a few others who asserted that only the oppressed should have the right to decide the language they wished to be addressed in. But if those were a few fanatics, they were also what the press and politicians gleefully picked up, first in the United States and then here as evidence of the Ultimate Threat. The truth about American PC is more complex but less glamorous. As Richard Gott, the literary editor of the *Guardian* – one of the few liberals who has attempted to explore this issue objectively – wrote when reviewing *Culture of Complaint: The Fraying of America* by Robert Hughes:

> [PC is] a notional construct put together by the Right to create a non-existent monster on the Left that it can then attack. For although everyone knows the idiocies uttered in the name of PC, it is hard to find anyone who has actually heard them in person or even encountered them seriously in print (except in the darkest corners of the obscurest journals). The American Left has long been conspicuous by its absence.[1]

Having created the Ultimate Threat, commentators and public figures felt free to let rip with the most rabid and cataclysmic language which they used to describe anything that questioned existing orthodoxies or iniquities. PC was evil, fascist, a witchhunt, the Cultural Revolution, the Plague, Stalinism, McCarthyism. It was also an invasion to be resisted here in England at all costs or, as Anne Leslie of the *Daily Mail*, a celebrated right-wing journalist, warned us in 1992 about the lethal carriers of this plague: 'They terrorize America and now they have established a beachhead on our shores.' Leslie, whose articles have become an almost one-woman guard against PC, predictably attacked the 1960s guilt-ridden camp for encouraging this menace. She must be overjoyed then to see how many of these wets have risen to her battlecry.

For once you know that your country needs you, like any good chap, whether on the right or the left, you march in there with the rest. And this is what has happened in Britain to an astonishing and depressing degree. Here, many on the left have been conspicuous not by their absence but by their collaboration with the forces of the right, eager to prove themselves more gutsy, less prone to that terrible white middle-class guilt that they believe so incapacitated them in the 1960s and 1970s. As the critic Patrick Wright says:

> [PC] provides the present day realist with a neat way of mocking every political and ethical challenge back into the obscurity of its corner while avoiding even the remotest engagement with its claims . . . it has become the reflex sneer of the Right that is no longer prepared to argue its case. However, it also has its attractions for refugees from the collapsing Left, stepping out from behind all that discarded ideological baggage to catch up with the opportunities of a world where everything seems to hang free.[2]

The real problem for me is not with such expedient people who, despite their pronouncements, always swim with the tide, but with those on the left with moral integrity and an impassioned belief in justice and equality – people like Melanie Phillips and Christopher Hitchens who appear in this book – who have joined the backlash. Why have so many such influential individuals fallen with relief into neo-liberal conservatism?

There are many possible reasons. Maybe it is that, as Norman Mailer says, human nature cannot bear very much change: 'The new always carries with it the sense of violation, of sacrilege. What is dead is sacred; what is new, that is different, is evil, dangerous, subversive.'[3] Or it could be that cultural, political and social equality is indeed a worthless or even perilous cause because the schisms it causes in a society in the end rebound on everyone, especially the original victims. Maybe these people are responding rationally to the collapse as they see it of all that they believed in and the inexorable rise and rise of the forces of opposition. This has impelled them, some for the sake of their sanity, to defect. Or it could be for reasons more cynical. That for these people the beliefs they once proclaimed were never really rooted, so that it was fine when change meant getting in a few anti-apartheid demos on a sunny day, applauding ethnic food and, for the truly radical, arranging for a token Black or Asian to get a few chances here and there. That, although they were just about able to go along with it, they were uncomfortable with the guilt, the constraints and most of all their potential disempowerment. That as soon as more was asked of them and they were charged with betrayal because they had done nothing to shift anything substantial, or where there was less pay-off because fewer Blacks seemed grateful and more spoke angrily of rights, then they withdrew with a vengeance.

It might also be that the generation which now holds power and influence is truly adrift. They cannot fall back on those anchors, the empire and the war, in the way their predecessors who had real experience of both, could. All they have are illusions about the great traditions of Western democracy and culture. The shedding of these and surrendering of a certain amount of power that PC demands is much too painful for those controlling a world that is already changing in ways that they cannot accept, especially from the positions they have occupied as if by divine right for so long.

You only need to look carefully at Christopher Hitchens' attack on PC in the *Independent on Sunday* on 13 June

1993 to see some of these sentiments and how these create what I would define as a web of myth making, defensive posturing and even wishful thinking. First he pays almost religious homage to the United States because it is 'par excellence, the land not just of free speech but of free expression'. Then he goes on to say – as if it is self-evident – that these freedoms mean that 'battles like those against bigotry and for women's suffrage are successful in the end' or that 'For the first time [in history] those who seek an extension of "rights" also argue for an abridgement of "speech".' Now none of this makes any sense to me. Does the fact that the principle of free speech is enshrined in the Constitution necessarily mean that it is a reality for all who live in the United States? Does Hitchens really believe that battles against bigotry have been successful? Tell that to all those waiting in soup queues and those whose talents will never be allowed to rise out of the desperate ghetto. Where in this analysis is the divided America that Galbraith so movingly described in his recent essay?[4] A man with the powerful intellect that Hitchens has should not make such unqualified statements. He must know that freedom, like choice, is entirely dependent on who you are. He must also know that the American dream is for many an illusion which saves the day when reality comes biting at the heels of the powerful. To those who are well fed and well placed the dream can remain real as long as the poor and excluded – whose levels of disease and deprivation now match many poor third world countries – don't make too much of a noise to wake them up.

For me, what Hitchens is really describing is the world of the privileged which in the United States is the majority. They must not be pushed so that they 'weary' of a good cause, they must not be confronted with sectarian pleading by some 'bunch of humourless citizens', they must never be 'repressed'. Those of us on the other side of the fence see a less idealised America than this, and for us there is perhaps a greater good than preserving the happiness and freedom of these people. As Galbraith says: 'In the good society there must not be a deprived and excluded underclass. There must be full democratic participation by all and from this alone can come a sense of community which accepts and even values diversity.'[5]

This is not to deride the United States. Many of the excellent developments that have taken place there in terms of curriculum changes in schools and pre-school education, where it is now a matter of course for all children to have a wide ranging multicultural education (something that it is impossible to imagine in this country now), happened because people took risks with the feelings of the all too easily wounded majority and argued that white and Black children were damaged by education which had assumed for generations that white is best and white men best of all. Research in both countries shows unequivocally that by the age of three Black and white children have a clear idea about racial categories and where they are placed on the hierarchy. Norbert Wiener, the American educationist, said back in the late 1950s: 'progress imposes not only new possibilities for the future, but new restrictions'.[6]

But restrictions, it seems to me, are unacceptable to these purveyors of free speech except when *they* impose them directly or indirectly on those whose views are infuriating because they are so illiberal. Simon Hoggart, who first transplanted the panic about PC to these shores, these days contents himself with imperiously passing judgement on which changes are acceptable and which ones anathema: 'Now that fire brigades are appointing women, "firefighters" isn't PC but is just accurate.'[7] Gee thanks. But, lectures Mr Hoggart, although PC has conspicuously failed to gain much ground here, constant vigilance is needed and to prove this we are given an extraordinary example. The *Sun* unusually and very effectively once devoted two pages to the issue of racism, using as its main example a story of a Black bridegroom who was thrown out of his honeymoon hotel because of his colour. This was not even of passing importance to Hoggart: 'The most interesting part of this exercise I thought was that it described the wronged groom as Afro-Caribbean which is the PC term for black.' So the real point of all this huffing and puffing is finally laid bare. In the eyes of powerful white men and women, racial injustice is less of an important issue to tackle than the new words they are having to mug up in order to be politically correct.

Now, thanks to the heroic work of Hoggart and others of his ilk, this burdensome yoke can be thrown off. In this newly liberated landscape we are getting some wonderful absurdities. Hoggart whinges that his children are bored with multicultural books – Lord help us that a white middle-class child should be *bored*. Such attitudes accost me fairly regularly at dinner parties because it is assumed that I am an expert in multiculturalism. On one such occasion, where we were discussing racial violence, someone who was 'in publishing' piped up, 'I think all this has been made worse by PC. It's destroying this country.' Encouraged by this, another guest confessed that he would not want his children to mix with too many ethnic minorities, 'No offence.' The host then added his bit about how stupid it was to be upset about children's books, and how we should return to basics. We rounded off the evening badly when I suggested to them that they had revealed how little they understood the world I came from, and how threatened they were by even the idea of a pluralistic equal society. They wanted to go 'back to basics' because it guaranteed them and their children their long-held privileged position and the literature they so passionately want to preserve feeds into that ambition. Why else would any parent want his/her child to read stuff like this by Enid Blyton: 'The face has nasty gleaming eyes and it looked very dark. Perhaps it was a black man's face. Oh I was so frightened'? Incidentally the Blyton passage was pointed out to me by a mother of a young Black boy who had tried to rub off his skin with a brillo pad.

Like it or not, these people have succeeded in pushing back the clock. They have forced a retreat from any progressive endeavour to such an extent that even Gus John, the black Director of Education at Hackney who has spent his life fighting for equal opportunities, when confronted with media madness over the case of Jane Brown, the excellent school head who made the admittedly stupid decision not to let pupils go to the ballet *Romeo and Juliet*, started talking about the 'fundamentalists' who needed to be disciplined. Jane Brown was foolish. But did she deserve vilification? Contrast this with the story of the vicar who wanted to burn women priests at the stake. Look how he was treated. He was not PC. He was not a threat to the nation. He was regarded as loopy, laughable even, just one of those eccentric men.

Anti-PC rhetoric has become a potent weapon, an

instant way of discrediting anybody who talks of the need for change, redress or equal rights. I do hope anti-PC warriors see the irony in this and recognise that *their* McCarthyism is much more like the real thing in that it is attacking imagined totalitarianism and it has the power to silence people. Never before have so many disenfranchised groups felt so undermined in the way their struggles for change have been treated by the intelligentsia and the body politic.

An example of this can be seen in the way anti-racist social work training has recently been attacked. Melanie Phillips, a journalist who has been an inspiration in the past with her brave and thoughtful writing, wrote this in a *news* piece in the *Observer* on 1 August 1993: 'University tutors are abandoning social work teaching because they say they are being forced to teach "politically correct" attitudes on race and gender in a climate of fear and intimidation.' Not all social work tutors of course, though Melanie Phillips fails to tell us how many she is talking about. And none who disagreed was interviewed for this news story which had several unnamed victims of this oppression and Professor Pinker of the London School of Economics arguing that institutional racism in Britain was simply a matter of opinion. What about all those reports by independent organisations like the Policy Studies Institute, NACRO, MIND, the Law Society which shows categorically that the judiciary, the medical profession, the police, the army, social work, etc., etc., operate in discriminatory ways? This report was augmented by a column by Phillips which continued in the same vein and was titled 'The Oppressors'. In the same week, Bryan Appleyard in the *Independent* came up with an almost identical column. The siege mentality was staggering.

The following week, in order to see if indeed these 'oppressors' were indeed as described, neo-Stalinists running amok, I interviewed 58 individuals across the country who were all enraged at the attacks on the changes that they believed were long overdue. The names included a professor at Edinburgh University, a head of department at Manchester Metropolitan University, and a member of the Medical Research Council. These people saw the need for training that prepared social workers to respond to a complicated, heterogeneous world where many clients experienced discrimination in their daily lives. How can this be wrong when we know there is over-representation of Black people in penal and care institutions? Sara, a white, very middle-class social worker, told me how the training helped her empathise with a young Black lone mother who was very isolated and very angry: 'I know without this insight I would have gone in with no idea what life was like for her. I would probably have patronised her and we would have got nowhere. I just went in and asked her how it felt to be Black on such a white estate. It was like a key opening.' And yet we had a situation where none of these voices of support were heard anywhere in the media.

Not surprisingly then, Virginia Bottomley has recently instructed the Central Council for Education and Training in Social Work to get rid of anti-racist training from the curriculum, in spite of the fact that all recent care legislation, including the Children Act and Care in the Community, makes it a statutory requirement for carers to consider the race and culture of clients. An employer who was committed to getting more women and ethnic minorities into the hierarchy was told by his head office he was to scrap the programme because it was PC and aimed at getting people positions simply because they were women or Black. Giving jobs to someone simply because they went to the same public school is still perfectly acceptable of course.

The power and fury of the anti-PC movement has also facilitated and excused the broader backlash against feminism and anti-racism. This is fast coming to be seen as the decade when feminism is finally dislodged, even destroyed, so men can feel good about the position they have always held. Look at the long line of men (and look also at the access they have had to the media) complaining (talk about culture of complaint) about how they have been emasculated by feminist zealots. Neil Lyndon, David Thomas, Warren Farrell, Robert Blythe, even Garrison Keeler, all weeping into their pages and demanding reinstatement of their manhood. That a prestigious organisation like PEN has joined in the protest against 'censorship' in children's books by anti-racists shows how retrogressive society has become. The same people would of course accept that we should not let our children read books that glamorise violence or promote sexuality.

Part of the backlash has also been the attack on what is seen as victim culture. This is the intellectual version of people talking about the sinful ways of those on benefits. The interesting thing is that it is those who have never suffered any real ongoing victimisation who have the most to say on what victims are and should be, how they should feel and behave. Disdain for victimhood is very trendy these days, allowing those in power to abandon all responsibility for the state of things. As Tagore said: 'Power takes as ingratitude the writhings of its victims.'

Another particular technique used by the left is to argue on behalf of victims. That they don't want to be tokens, or that it is demeaning for them to be patronised by positive action, or that if they carry on in this way the resentment of the masses will lead to a real attack on them by the right in some remote future. Well, speaking for myself, I would love to be a token in some white power bastion, because tokenism is the first step to change. As for the terrible right, at least I know the animal and anyway, I can't see how much they could do to me that the left isn't already doing extremely well. But then victims are also naïve I suspect.

Finally and perhaps most dangerously of all, the PC backlash has given a new credibility to a kind of cultural protectionism where the intellectual legacy can admit no challenge. The idea that existing culture is neutral and God given is patently nonsense. Yet this is what is seriously argued by men who know. In his radical book *Beyond the Culture Wars: How Teaching the Conflicts can Revitalise American Education*, Gerald Graff tackles this by dispelling the paranoia about classics being burnt in funeral pyres on American campuses and also rejecting the idea of an all-embracing, disinterested value system. He believes (rightly) that disrespect for and debate about traditional cultural edifices by those on the margins is important for the whole of society.

There are deeper implications in all this. The pillar of Western civilisation, secular liberalism, has shown that it cannot live up to its own cherished ideals. Liberals do not allow real confrontations with liberalism. Theirs is a carefully circumscribed world within which you can dance any dance you like but within their space and to their tune. There was a time when they were prepared to look critically at their world. Those days are gone. A blindness has set in. Intelligent people seriously argue that they are protecting their precious freedom of speech in a country where the rich can curtail it through the libel laws, where gagging clauses now appear in virtually any important job people are involved in and where editors quite deliberately choose to disallow certain points of view.

The days are also gone when all minorities were asking for was a slice of the cake. They now seek greater transformations. All this is happening in a political climate where for more than a decade Thatcher and Reagan destroyed many of the foundations of equal opportunity and civil rights developments. Any kind of collectivist action was considered archaic or deranged. Problems were attributed to individual failure. Success was measured in terms of how many Bill Cosbys one could find. One can hardly be surprised if the decade also produced some extremists and separatists who no longer had any faith in the system. Sometimes it is hard to decide who the wise are, those who still cling to the hope of change or those who have turned away.

The global restructuring that has been taking place is also having an impact. On the one hand the new cultural jingoism is a by-product of triumphalism that has followed in the wake of the collapse of communism. The West has won the economic and political battles of the twentieth century. It follows naturally then that Western culture too must rest again where it once did during colonialism. Read the pride with which Mary Kenny writes this in the *Daily Telegraph* in 1992: 'It only requires the most superficial stroll through the National Gallery, the Louvre or the corridors of the Vatican to see the evidence before your eyes that western art is indeed an extraordinary phenomenon which has never been matched by any other culture.'

It may be of course that this kind of tub-thumping and the rise of fundamentalist liberalism is the result not of hubris but unease at the profound changes that are going on in the world. Too many natives are restless and not prepared to acquiesce any longer. Some, like the Muslims, have, through their protests against *The Satanic Verses*, challenged every assumption on art and life that has hitherto been sacred, exposing how the liberals too have their god. And a jealous God theirs is too which refuses to understand the faith of others. They would not accept the validity of the deep sense of offence that most Muslims felt – and here I am not talking about the fatwa which came out of a theocracy in Iran and has nothing to do with British Muslims. In fact the Muslim outrage itself gave some people licence to malign and attack them further, though as a result of those protests there is at least, thank God, a wider debate about the limits to and responsibilities of freedom.

Intellectuals from around the world are beginning to ask important questions about the values of a culture which is dominated by Hollywood, Coca-Cola and Murdoch on the one hand and imperialistic liberalism on the other. Why is it obligatory to opt for values which not only expunge other viable alternatives, but have resulted in the West struggling with its own demons? This is how the Indian intellectual Ashis Nandy describes what the new fight for independence is all about:

> Many non-Western observers of the culture of the modern West – its lifestyle, literature, arts and its human sciences – have been struck by the way contracted competitive individualism – and the utter loneliness that flows from it – dominates Western mass

society. From Friedrich Nietzsche to Karl Marx, to Franz Kafka, much of Western social analysis, too, has stood witness to this cultural pathology. What once looked like independence from one's immediate authorities in the family, and a defiance of the larger aggregates they represented, now looks more and more like a Hobbesian world view gone rabid.[8]

Ziauddin Sardar, a Muslim writer, has similar thought-provoking opinions in his book, *Distorted Imagination*,[9] which he co-wrote with Merryl Win Davis in response to the Rushdie crisis:

> 'Civilization as we know it' has always meant Western civilization. Civilized behaviour and products have been measured by the yardsticks of the West. Europe and now North America has always contemplated itself as the focus of the world, the axis of civilization, the goal of history, the end product of human destiny. Colonial history and colonial Christianity did their utmost both to annihilate non-Western cultures and obliterate their histories. Now secularism in its post modernist phase of desperate self glorification has embarked on the same goal.

These are important explorations necessary to wake us all from our complacent slumbers and to expose the lies we tell ourselves. For those of us on the outside, we know now that integration on our terms is something that is more complex and harder to achieve than we imagined. We have also acquired scepticism. We are less easily flattered and placated by white praise and less wounded by white displeasure. We have learned that fighting for a more just and multifarious world needs not only this scepticism, but courage to remain steadfast whatever torrents we face. In order to do that, we need to make allies, and deal with our own destructive impulses and antediluvian cultural practices. We need to remind the world that words matter. In the words of Professor Alexander Bickett of Yale University: 'Where nothing is unspeakable, nothing is undoable.' We need to be prepared to engage in this massive confrontation with the West – whilst acknowledging how we too are part of it – so that the non-white world is allowed to be authentic and properly established within an expanding canon and where there is genuine diversity and equality in politics, society and culture. We need, for example, to reinstate lost history for all our sakes. Telling people that five million Indians and a million Caribbeans volunteered to fight in the two world wars is vital so that all our children may learn to recognise how many of us truly 'belong' here. Liberals will need to engage in a much more dynamic and self-critical relationship with those who inhabit different cultural worlds and give them genuine access and status. The common good that people are seeking will come not out of denying that inequality and difference exist but by dealing with the first and embracing the second.

As Ben Okri said in his perceptive essay on *Othello*: 'ultimately we are bound in fate with whoever the other may be. We are bound in the fact that we have to deal with one another. There's no way around it . . . The way we see the other is connected to the way we see ourselves. The other is ourselves as the stranger.'[10]

NOTES

1 *Guardian*, 1 June 1993.
2 *Guardian*, 1 June 1993.
3 'With Edgard Varèse in the Gobi Desert', *The Air-conditioned Nightmare*, Secker & Warburg, 1945.
4 'Towards a New World Deal', *Guardian*, 26 January 1994.
5 Ibid.
6 *The Human Use of Human Beings: Cybernetics and Society*, Eyre & Spottiswoode, 1950.
7 *Observer*, 11 July 1993.
8 'Cultural Frames for Social Transformation', *Alternatives*, vol. II:1, 1987.
8 9 *Distorted Imagination: Lessons from the Rushdie Affair*, Grey Seal Books, 1990.
10 'Leaping out of Shakespeare's Terror: Five Meditations on *Othello*', *Storms of the Heart*, ed. Kwesi Owusu, Camden Press, 1988.

Linda Grant

SEX AND THE SINGLE STUDENT: THE STORY OF DATE RAPE

In the mid-1970s, a woman who had just arrived in a strange city to take up a place in a university graduate programme was invited to dinner. The hostess lived in an outlying suburb. The woman was not familiar with the city's layout or how to get there but managed, with some trouble, to negotiate her way by bus – a lengthy journey. She had been promised that one of the guests, one of her new fellow graduate students, would drive her home, a kind offer since he too lived in that distant suburb and the journey was definitely out of his way.

The woman did not particularly like the man. She thought him arrogant and pompous. She was also dismayed by how much he drank. Finally, well after three, he rose to leave. It was immediately apparent as soon as they set off that he was very drunk, far too drunk to drive and the woman did not drive herself. The man readily agreed that he should not be behind the wheel and he suggested that as he lived only a short distance away, they should go to his flat where she could spend the night and he would drive her home in the morning. The woman was extremely relieved. It did not occur to her that once at his flat, she could call a cab. Taxis were outside the realm of experience of students on a state grant. She knew they *existed*, she had been in them, with her parents. But taking a taxi, then, was the equivalent of the budget traveller flying first class.

In his living room, he put on some music and poured two more glasses of brandy. Although his flat was in a soulless, modern block, it had a balcony and he took her out on to it to see the lights of the city in the distance. He put his arm on her shoulder and she let it lie there, too tired and embarrassed to think of anything to say. At last she found her tongue and told him she must sleep. He took her into a bedroom with a double bed. 'This is your room,' he said and she assumed there must be another. She quickly got between the sheets and in a matter of minutes, she was asleep. Almost immediately, she heard the door open and felt him in the room, undressing and getting in beside her. 'Isn't there another bedroom?' she asked. 'No,' he said. 'This is my room.'

She told him that she was very tired and she did not

want to make love. She said this politely at first. She tried saying it every way she could think of but he ignored her. He wasn't listening. By now he was lying on top of her. Out of the corner of her eye she saw, by the side of the bed, a set of weight-training equipment. The heavily muscled man on top of her was, she realised, physically quite unlike any other men she knew, the pale hippies of those days with their long hair and pipe-cleaner arms whose sole form of exercise was striking a match against the box to light another joint.

She made one more effort to tell him that she wanted to sleep but he just smiled and ignored her. 'Oh Christ,' she thought. 'Okay, okay, let's just get it over with.' He ground away for a very long time. She lay there thinking, 'Please, let him come. Let him finish.' Finally he collapsed suddenly and fell asleep on top of her. She pushed and pushed but he would not budge. She lay awake for several hours under him until, at around ten, the phone rang and she thought she was free. He slept through it. It rang again an hour later and after many rings, he answered it. It was his girlfriend. He was supposed to be driving her to the country for the day. Where was he?

The woman was living in a shared house she had found in an advertisement on the campus noticeboard. She had known none of her housemates for longer than a few days but she was so angry and fed up she told the first person she met in the kitchen what had happened. 'You've been raped,' that person said.

Not long afterwards, she read Susan Brownmiller's recently published landmark book, *Against Our Will: Men, Women and Rape*,[1] from which she learned that rape was not an isolated crime committed by an individual suffering from a particular sexual pathology but an aspect of male power and male violence, with a long and fascinating history. While she never believed the popular slogan of the time, 'all men are rapists', she saw that all men were potentially rapists. She gave a great deal of thought to the nature of consent. She was able to see how much sex she had was not wanted by her but often she did not have the terms on which to decline. Crippled by politeness and by women's traditional fear of arousing a man's anger by refusing him what he wants, she said yes when she meant no, a far more usual reversal of what men thought women's hidden message was. In those fading days of the sexual revolution, this redefinition of rape gave considerable empowerment. The woman found that she was able to use it on subsequent occasions. 'I've told you no,' she would say. 'Are you going to rape me?'

What did the woman do next? By the end of the afternoon she'd pretty well forgotten about the night before. She did not feel defiled. She did not shower a dozen times, scrubbing at her skin. She did not feel her identity evaporate. She did not call the police. She did not inform the university authorities. She did not confront the man. What she did do was to tell a number of people what had happened and it was agreed that it was typical of him – he was an egocentric, arrogant bastard; that was the consensus. Everyone felt sorry for his girlfriend but no one told her. No one suggested the woman should go for counselling. No one held her. She didn't develop an eating disorder and she was never afterwards able to feel that the event was a trauma. She just had it down as a bad night.

★

Of course it was me that this happened to, but it is often worth turning our subjective experiences into objective events, the better to understand them. A woman returns to a man's flat late at night, a man she has only met a few hours before. The man is drunk, she is not sober. They stand on the balcony admiring a romantic view, a glittering cityscape. He has his arm around her and she does not remove it. She gets into his bed. She does not scream the place down when he tries to have sex with her. She lets it happen. She is very far from being virginal. She has had plenty of one-night stands. Both parties to the incident are students, notorious for their disorderly conduct. The next day she feels no great ill-effects from her 'ordeal'. She does not report the incident but she does try to blacken his name. She defines herself as having been raped.

In her book *The Morning After: Sex, Fear and Feminism on Campus*,[2] Katie Roiphe expresses astonishment with the statistic that alleges one in four women have been raped. 'If 25 per cent of my women friends had been raped, wouldn't I know?' she asks. In this I disagree strongly with Roiphe. The extent of date rape is only now coming to be known and may be even greater than that figure. Ask around and one discovers how many women who are sexually active have been raped in this way. British rape statistics indicate that between 60 and 70 per cent of rapists are known to their victims. Look into the history of marriage and one finds women whose entire married lives consisted of nothing but rape on a regular basis by drunken husbands asserting their 'rights'. Whether or not Lorena Bobbitt was abused and violently sexually assaulted by her husband, John Bobbitt, the response of many women to her removal of his penis reflects the true depths of female anger against male violence which floods the world not only with its actions but with its images.

Many, many women have been raped in circumstances very similar to those described above. They found themselves in a situation, they could not find a way of getting out of it and it was easier to stay silent, to let it just happen than to attempt a futile struggle. At universities and colleges, within a closed society of friends, there are ways of taking one's revenge. But now the political climate has changed and if that event which happened in the mid-1970s had occurred today, the man would possibly have lost his place in the graduate programme and the future of literary criticism would have been . . . well, let's be charitable . . . all the poorer. The woman would have been positively encouraged by women's groups on campus to speak out about her ordeal and it would naturally have been assumed that she would require counselling. The press, on the other hand, would be howling about political correctness, about the menace of feminism, and though the woman would have been unnamed, she would still have been vilified in the tabloids.

The question, then, is not whether date rape is a significant phenomenon – it clearly is and always has been – but why it has assumed such importance in the 1990s. If there is nothing new about date rape, particularly at universities, then what *is* new is the panic it has engendered on both sides of the debate. What has changed in 15 years? Were those who were date raped in the past and suffered no consequent trauma, 'in denial' as the fashionable theory currently has it? Why has the accusation of date rape turned into such a menace? Why have women's issues been burdened with so much responsibility for what has come to be defined as the gagging of intellectual life, the overthrow of liberal, humanistic civilisation as we know it? How has feminism been turned into the American equivalent of Islamic fundamentalism, ruled over by a few mad 20-year-old mullahs at Harvard and Princeton? Is this spectre of date rape PC any kind of issue at all in Britain or are we summoning up a foreign bogy to frighten ourselves with? And finally, why is feminism so fixated on rape, pornography and incest when the great issues of 1960s and 1970s feminism – equal pay, workplace nursery provision, proper rights for part-time employees – remain largely unresolved? How have these economic issues come to seem so unutterably boring in the minds of most feminists?

In part, of course, the growing awareness of date rape has been aided by the number of cases that reach the courts, particularly those which involve celebrities such as Mike Tyson or William Kennedy Smith. The guarantee of anonymity in court introduced in 1976 in Britain and the redefinition of the law to include rape inside marriage in 1991 have emboldened many women to prosecute who would not have done so before even though rape is one of the most under-reported crimes. Every successful prosecution spawns many more. The British media, looking for its own homegrown versions of notable American ones, ensures maximum publicity for each case. Even so, the Diggle case in 1993 was particularly spectacular because it was so clear-cut. Diggle and his victim were on an actual date of the most traditional kind: a St Andrew's Day Ball at which he even paid for his partner. Diggle was not some shadowy psychopath but a solicitor, albeit one with a sad fantasy life.

The fact that these debates have been most fierce in the

United States should not come as a surprise. America was constitutionally founded on the notion of 'rights'; it is embedded deep in the political consciousness. Over the past decade the middle class in America have come to see, in the fallout of the political activism of the 1960s, the potency of the politics of rights. Black rights, women's rights, gay rights – there is no percentage in being amongst the guilty and one senses how many Americans are now scrambling to acquire the status of a victim perpetually in recovery from some malaise or other. And if colleges like Harvard and Princeton are, according to Roiphe, such a hotbed of concern about date rape is it not that passionate, committed middle-class students have found a victim status they can readily identify with? Is date rape as big an issue in the community colleges of the Midwest?

But there are other, less obvious reasons for the way date rape dominates the politics of the campuses. In the 1990s, sexual politics is pretty much all that activists have left to be active about. The ascendancy of the right from the election of Thatcher and Reagan onwards, the mutilation of the trade union movement, the disintegration of opposition parties and the failure of revolutions in Nicaragua and El Salvador – all have enfeebled classic left-wing organising in the 1980s. The last strike of any significance in Britain involving women workers, the Grunwick dispute in which Asian women stubbornly tried to unionise their workplace, was a defeat. The firing of the air traffic controllers early in Reagan's presidency demoralised the labour movement in the US. The destruction of the GLC in the mid-1980s and the sustained attack on town hall socialism eliminated most of the possibilities for grass-roots political action. There was little scope for activists to *do* anything.

Now politics, as we know, abhors a vacuum. People with a political consciousness don't just go away and do something else because they don't know how to fight. The poverty is still there, the injustice is still there. They still see it. They still feel it. Feminism and sexual politics have been one of the few arenas in which political gains continue to be made and it should not surprise us if a new generation of committed students sees in rape a sexual power struggle which is fought over every day, in their own lives.

Until feminism, student politics had been a playpen in which one had a chance to act out the issues of the real world outside the campus. By the 1980s, feminism had begun to look at the relations between men and women within the universities and that gave student politics an enormous power it had not had before. Campuses became test sites for every theory about relations between the sexes, between the races and between the sexualities. It is little wonder that student politics has reached out and been recognised well beyond the bounds of campuses themselves. Student politics have proved to be far from impotent.

Still, the opponents of the 'rape crisis feminists', as they have been dubbed by Roiphe, seem to me to be rightly alarmed by the way in which the issue of date rape (and other forms of sexual violence such as pornography and incest) has come to blot out everything else in the sky. The ambiguity of the sexual encounter is inevitably prone to misinterpretation. A date, in and of itself, as Camille

Paglia has pointed out, is an opportunity for both parties to size each other up sexually. 'Sex is hovering in the air,' she writes. 'Hover, hover, hover.'[3] The attempt by students at Antioch College, Ohio, to create written agreements at each stage of the sexual encounter is implausible, unworkable. Sex isn't like that and, as Roiphe observes, do we *want* to take all the sense of danger out of such an encounter?

As the novelist Mary Gaitskell recently argued in the American magazine *Harpers*,[4] discussing her own experience of date rape:

> One reason I had sex with strangers when I really didn't want to was that part of me wanted the adventure, and that tougher part ran roughshod over the part of me that was scared and uncertain. I'll bet the same thing happened to many of the boys with whom I had these experiences. All people have their tough, aggressive selves as well as their more delicate selves.

Do we honestly believe in a futureworld without the madness of passion? Will we ever rid campuses of drugs, drink and bonking? One British student told a journalist: 'We all know each other, we all have hormones, very little money and not many responsibilities. What else do you expect?'

In the rhetoric against rape crisis feminism there has been little discussion of the real weakness in the date rape argument: that all rapes are equal, all equally traumatic. I want to argue here a point which many will find uncomfortable: that if we look at rape closely enough, we may find not so much a hierarchy of rape, but that there are significant differences in the way women experience rape and that those who seem less traumatised than others are not necessarily suffering from a form of what used to be called false consciousness. The lack of trauma does not make the rape less wrong, but understanding the role of rape within the context of other traumas, I believe, sheds light on why sexual assault has become such a significant political movement on campuses.

First, as Katie Roiphe has eloquently pointed out, the discourse of rape testimonies at American universities and elsewhere has taken on an eerie, Orwellian Newspeak language: the ritual invocation of the breaking of a silence, the rape's removal of the victim's self-esteem, her sense of shame and defilement, her eventual movement 'into recovery'. 'Somehow', Roiphe writes,

> the individual power of each story is sapped by the collective mode of expression. The individual details fade, the stories blend together, sounding programmed and automatic . . . As intimate details are squeezed into formulaic standards, they seem to be wrought with an emotion more generic than heartfelt . . . With its candles, its silence, its promise of transformations, this movement offers a substitute for religion.

So let's compare the ritualised rape confession at an American university with rape in an entirely different sphere. The reason why rape as a war crime became such an issue in Bosnia is because the war in the former Yugoslavia was the first conflict to be witnessed by a modern, sophisticated and well-developed women's movement. Feminist organisations in Zagreb, capital of Croatia, began very early on to accumulate accounts of rape.

One, Tresnjevka, was the first organisation to document *how* rape takes place in wartime. The Red Cross, which could offer no statistics on this subject, admitted that for a woman to report rape she would have to go to see a male officer and talk to him probably through a male interpreter. An international movement sprang up to reclassify rape as a war crime within the Geneva Convention. European and American feminists began to take the risky journey to the Balkans to try to provide rape counselling. Psychiatrists in Bosnia and Croatia admitted they had no experience of this kind of work. But when projects began to be set up in Bosnia specifically targeted at counselling women who had been raped, they found the unexpected.

Many of the women they spoke to did not see rape as their primary trauma. They had lost their homes, seen husbands taken away and killed; they had been bombed and separated from their children. Their sons were away fighting. 'When the men come back from the front line they tend to be alienated, there's a lot of alcoholism and violence and so the women are asking how they can cope with situations like that,' one social worker said. 'There's great concern for their men folk and their behaviour swings.' One of the great double whammies about the traumatised male is the extent to which his own hurt exerts a power way beyond himself. What these women are saying is that their husbands and sons returning from the war with their own traumas exert a greater trauma on the women than the rape she might have experienced. The rape is over. The rapist is gone. But the men that they married or gave birth to have turned into monsters, and that is an ongoing situation.

The response of the Muslim world was also a factor in

how they dealt with the rape. For the young women in less sophisticated rural areas, it was necessary for them to be virgins if they were to find husbands. Defiled, would no one want them? Religious leaders decided that they were not responsible for their condition and informed followers of the faith that they should be treated as war heroines.

There is a parallel in peacetime with rapes that happen in war and that is the largely unconsidered issue of the rape of the elderly. Rapes of older women generally take place in the following way: a man, usually many years younger than the victim, forcibly enters her home. He threatens or carries out physical violence, steals money or jewellery and leaves her where she may not be found for hours or even days if she lives alone. Women who are now in their seventies and eighties married during the 1930s and 1940s when there were strong pressures on women to be virgins until their wedding night. Reaching the menopause as the sexual revolution began in the early 1960s, they are likely to have had only one sexual partner throughout their lives. Those who are widowed may not have had any sexual contact for many years. The menopause itself dehydrates the vagina making penetrative sex, even when desired, often painful. All in all, rape for an elderly woman should be particularly traumatic.

It may be shocking but in fact the opposite seems to be true. What little research there is indicates that elderly women cope better with the aftermath of rape than younger ones. When questioned, they often cite other traumas during the course of their lifetimes as being worse: the experience of the last war, losing a father, being widowed. But more importantly, they do not suffer what is known as 'secondary trauma' – the attitude of society to the victim. Like women who are raped in wartime, old women are not accused of somehow having 'asked for it' by wearing sexy clothes or behaving in a provocative manner. They are not expected to have tried to fight off their attacker. Society – even mullahs in mosques in Zagreb – does not put that extra pressure on to them. And crucially for older women, such is the disgust that society as a whole feels about sex and the elderly, the rapist is assumed to be somehow 'abnormal'. All in all older women are not tormented by the thoughts that somehow they provoked the assault and were in part to blame.

These different kinds of experience, I believe, shed a certain light on the whole date rape debate. First, as I have already stressed, they challenge the notion that rape is rape is rape, to be experienced by all women equally in exactly the same manner. Rapes that are far more serious and attended by greater physical violence are sometimes less traumatic than date rape and this should give us a clue as to why date rape continues to dominate the discourse of feminist politics on campus.

One reason is to do with the pathology of trauma. Mary Gaitskell was raped twice, once by a boy with whom she was at college, the second time by an attacker who repeatedly said he was going to kill her. Gaitskell was less traumatised by the second rape: 'I realise that the observation seems bizarre,' she writes,

> but for me the rape was a clearly defined act, perpetrated on me by a crazy asshole whom I didn't know or trust; it had nothing to do with me or who I was, and so, when it was over, it was relatively easy to

dismiss. Emotional cruelty is more complicated. Its motives are often impossible to understand, and it is sometimes committed by people who say they like or even love you.

The students who have invested so much energy into the issue of date rape are young women, away from home for the first time, uncertain. For many who have led a happy, secure childhood, rape absolutely *is* the worst thing that has ever happened to them. Unlike elderly women, they are still in the process of constructing their identities, still learning how to have intimate relationships with others. The fragility of their social identities is underscored by society's view of them, a microcosm of the emotional cruelty meted out to women in general; no longer under Daddy's protection, they are now culpable sexual figures in their own right. An apparently wanton cruelty bestowed by a boy one has thought was familiar but has turned into a menacing stranger must seem terrifying and surely must feel like a colossal betrayal, returning you to square one in your assessment of who these people are, all around you, and why they behave the way they do.

And of course date rape is happening at a time of massive anxiety about sexuality. My own date rape took place when sexual relations were astonishingly informal and when sex was momentarily freed from a whole set of traditional anxieties. It was very possible to separate sex from everything else: from pregnancy, from disease and from love; and equally possible for a woman who had been date raped to feel that the incident was simply one more example of what there was in abundance at the time – bad sex. Women were only just in the process of exploring and owning their own desires. The new understanding of rape which was coming into being then gave women the confidence to move beyond the first stage of empowerment the sexual revolution offered: the permission to say yes without the loss of one's reputation and, given the pill and legal abortion, without the great possibility of pregnancy. The second stage of the sexual revolution, beginning in the mid-1970s and fuelled by authors such as Brownmiller, involved consciousness of one's desires sufficient to allow one to say no.

But now sex has become the site of danger and, as Katie Roiphe argues, 'some of the attention lavished on the darker, violent side of sex comes from a deep ambivalence about what [sexual] freedom actually entails'. Inevitably, AIDS has induced a massive retreat from the casual freedoms of the 1960s and 1970s. But it has also complicated what are already difficult issues about growing up as a young woman today. Girls are issued with sets of conflicting messages: have sex and AIDS is likely to kill them, but they must look sexy if they are to catch a man because nothing has changed in that respect; the kind of postfeminism inspired by Madonna says they must know their own desires, act on them, be raunchy, be in control; yet campuses still resound with taunts of the 'college slut' for every girl who tries to follow Madonna's lead. The problem with Madonna as a role model is that she is above what society says because it is easy not to give a toss when you are sitting on her mountain of self-earned personal wealth.

The two date rape cases in 1993 involving students provided such an insight into the lives of young women at British universities today. The woman who failed in her attempt to prosecute Matthew Kydd, a 21-year-old student in Norwich, had already been nicknamed 'Slut of the Year' on her campus. On the one hand, we were told, she had played strip poker with two men she had picked up at a nightclub. On the other, she had expected that she would be able to have *non-penetrative* (i.e. safe) sex with Kydd. The world in which Madonna acts out her sexual fantasies did not operate for this young woman. The other actors would not obey the rules.

This sense of treachery was well-expressed in the Donnallan case. Austen Donnallan, a London University student, was facing a university disciplinary inquiry which could have ended in his expulsion. Convinced of his innocence, he insisted that the matter be taken to the police, though the woman herself had specifically requested that it should not go to court. Donnallan was acquitted, having had character references from several other female students. After the acquittal, the woman insisted that she still believed she had been raped: 'I never said I didn't kiss Austen, but a kiss is just a kiss; ask any student', she told journalists. The basis of her argument was that she was so drunk she was unconscious, a 'semi-comatose vegetable'. One senses here a sexuality swinging about through a set of rules everyone is misconstruing: 'A student code is unique and, I suppose, difficult for others to understand', she would later say. 'I realise now this is not foolproof and it is perhaps safer to stick to more conventional rules.' What caused her to insist that the matter be taken further? Rage, of course. But also because young women today cannot shrug and walk away from bad sex. Rape has the potential to be a far more lethal cocktail than a boring night of boring and embarrassment in the hallways for the next few weeks. The memory of it is a terror. Sex is freighted with negative consequences which the intelligent know they must confront. The morning after you don't just ask 'Am I pregnant?' (which you can do something about if you wish) but 'Has he given me a fatal disease?' You cannot simply wake up with a hangover and forget about the whole business. Bad sex follows you about these days. And there is a further imperative placed on the raped woman that did not exist for those who had not read Susan Brownmiller back in 1977. Feminism has imposed expectations on those who are committed to sexual politics. If you are a feminist and you have been raped, you do something about it because the mechanisms exist by which to speak out. The feminist I was in the 1970s would undoubtedly have reported my date rape had today's consciousness of sexual violence existed then.

My own view is that rape is a more complex phenomenon than the feminists of American universities believe it to be. It deserves to be treated with greater detached intellectual inquiry and fewer slogans. But do I fear the power of their simplistic assumptions? Do I believe that political correctness will swamp and destroy the gains that feminism has made in the past two decades?

The problem with revolutions is that they are, by definition, very rarely bloodless. Radical change has always attracted zealots for it is only those who see the world in black and white terms who can successfully initiate and sustain action. 'On the one hand, but then again on the other hand' has never been an effective rallying cry. Slogans do have the effect of cutting through doubt and arousing people's passions, giving them an easy way of identifying personal injustice. And it is, after all, students who are the cutting edge of the date rape debate. Adolescents have all the bright passionate qualities needed of radicals – they are single-minded, they see things in black and white, they want to act rather than to think about acting. They also tend to lack the compassion and humility about others' motives which creep up on you in old age like a curse to destroy your certainties.

One of the most remarkable books written about revolutions is Vivian Gornick's *The Romance of American Communism*,[5] which followed up the lives of America's communists after they had left the party. Many spoke of political correctness, a term which seems to have its origins in the democratic centralism of communism. They spoke of the recriminations against those who did not follow the party line, of the internal trials and the expulsions which echoed the McCarthy hearings. Gornick herself left the party in the mid-1950s and was not an activist again until 1968 when she became caught up in the second wave of feminism.

'And then the unthinkable happened to the women's movement: feminist consciousness began to give way to feminist dogma,' she writes. 'A militant rhetoric developed, an ideology began to form, a hard-edged theory of revolution flourished, "correct" and "incorrect" attitudes were defined, and bitter factional schisms occurred in the major feminist organisations.' For the first time she saw what had destroyed the Communist Party and at the same time she realised the great power of its ideas and influences:

> The second wave of American feminism never did become the property of the women's movement. On the contrary: it proved to have a life of its own with the power to influence thought and behaviour in the world far beyond the control of the movement. There are today thousands of people in the United States who do not call themselves feminists and do not know what is going on in feminist circles in New York, Boston or Berkeley whose lives are nevertheless profoundly changed by feminist consciousness.

Much as I abhor the stultifying discourse of all ideological correctnesses, we have to take the long view. The panic about date rape will in due course subside and students will, inevitably, find some other new cause to move on to. Meanwhile, far, far away from Harvard, Princeton and Yale, the effects will quietly and unseen by columnists and pundits take their course. Men and women will try to work out new ways of communicating. They will experiment with different forms in which to negotiate the old, old move from a glance across a room to bed. All this is taking place already. When asked what constitutes sexual harassment most younger men are well aware that a pat on the behind or a stroke of the breast in an office situation does not constitute professional behaviour. The signals, after a time of confusion, are getting clearer and it should not be necessary for written consent before one gets a member of the opposite sex into a compromising position.

And we will have those mad, bad muddled date rape feminists to thank for it – who will be older and will cringe with embarrassment when they remember what they used to think, what they used to say.

NOTES

1 Simon & Schuster, USA, 1975.
2 Hamish Hamilton, 1994.
3 *Sex, Art and American Culture: Essays*, Penguin, 1993.
4 March 1994.
5 Basic Books, 1977.

Lisa Jardine

CANON TO LEFT OF THEM, CANON TO RIGHT OF THEM

For the first lecture of my first-year Shakespeare course in the Department of English at Queen Mary and Westfield College, University of London, the set play is *Othello*. There are two early versions of the play, dating from 1622 (the quarto) and 1623 (the first folio); these versions differ substantially. In my lecture I show how every modern editor of the play has made different decisions in choosing words, phrases, even scene divisions from these two versions and combining them in a single 'definitive' text of the play. In order to see how dramatically different the same play can turn out in different editors' hands the students are asked to bring any paperback edition of *Othello* with them to the lecture. That way they can see how the book they hold, and treat with such reverence as *the* definitive version of the play, silently makes its choices. We can then discuss what difference it makes to our understanding of the play to find, for example, that in Act 4, scene 3 of the play, Emilia's speech asserting female independence and women's right to stand up to their husbands is in one surviving version of *Othello* but not in the other.

That, at least, is how my opening lecture was planned to go. But my introductory Shakespeare lecture produced a more unexpected discovery than simply that editorial tinkering with texts can alter the lasting relevance of a particular play. It was as a result of taking four different paperback editions of *Othello* home and reading through their lengthy introductions to prepare my lecture that it dawned on me (but only slowly) that in every one of the editions we were looking at the twentieth-century editor makes the tacit assumption that the reader of the play-text is white.

What I mean is the following. All the introductions to modern editions of *Othello* are reasonably sophisticated in their treatment of race in the play. They devote considerable space to presenting available evidence on the presence (or rather, for the most part, the absence) of Africans and Arabs in England in the late sixteenth and early seventeenth centuries. They assemble contemporary comment on race and attitudes to 'aliens' so as to give an idea of the extent of racial prejudice. They mark the distance between our own more or less enlightened attitudes and the way an infrequent encounter like the embassy from Barbary led by Abd el-Ouahed ben Messaoud 'troubled' the court in 1600, while their dress, customs and behaviour 'caused a scandal' in London.[1] Nevertheless, at the end of such learned discussion, each editor positions us, the readers of the edition, with the Venetians. Sensitive as the discussion of race tends increasingly to be, the readers who carefully resist Elizabethan stereotypical responses are unhesitatingly white, while the play's hero, Othello, is 'other'.

Of course, nowadays, we all ritually throw up our hands in horror at the way race is handled in the Arden edition of the play, edited by M. R. Ridley, and reprinted continuously, without modification, since it was first issued in 1958. There, famously, the apologies offered for Othello are unashamedly racist; Othello is a 'negro', but of a reassuringly *nice* kind:

> Now a good deal of trouble arises, I think, from a confusion of colour and contour. To a great many people the word 'negro' suggests at once the picture of what they would call a 'nigger', the woolly hair, thick lips, round skull, blunt features, and burnt-cork blackness of the traditional nigger minstrel . . . There are more races than one in Africa, and that a man is black in colour is no reason why he should, even in European eyes, be sub-human. One of the finest heads I have ever seen on any human being was that of a negro conductor on an American Pullman car. He had lips slightly thicker than an ordinary European's, and he had somewhat curly hair; for the rest he had a long head, a magnificent forehead, a keenly chiselled nose, rather sunken cheeks, and his expression was grave, dignified, and a trifle melancholy. He was coal-black, but he might have sat to a sculptor for a statue of

> Caesar, or, as far as appearance went, have played a superb Othello.[2]

Such comments betray the most obvious and unreflecting racism. It ought to give us pause for thought that this edition is still in print, and available in every High Street bookshop. But in a funny sort of way, Ridley can be dealt with nowadays by simple mockery. Ridley wrote within a few years of the beginning of an organised government policy of Caribbean and Asian immigration, designed to provide cheap labour in this country, which permanently altered the ethnic mix of Britain.[3] The gap between Ridley's naïvely racist language and our own is so evident, so stilted and dated, that we are easily able to separate ourselves from it, to disclaim responsibility for it and shrug it off as a relic from a bygone era. (We might however ask ourselves why it has apparently proved so difficult to find a scholar who is prepared to re-edit the Arden *Othello* – does the obviousness of the old edition's racism mean that re-editing smacks of policing the text?)

The students in my lecture hall were not all white. When I registered the unexpected way in which they were accidentally excluded from the introductory discussion of the play to which I had referred them I felt it only right to offer them an apology. Worse, however, was to come. For no Afro-Caribbean or Asian student had registered (as far as I have been able to establish) that they were not addressed by their editor. They were, after all, entirely used to the idea that the books they picked up in the classroom were designed for students other than themselves. I was simply voicing concern over something they had learned to live with, something which in some real sense *defined* their participation in our educational system

– participants, but not participants on precisely the same terms as 'ordinary' or 'traditional' students. In this respect nothing much has changed since the great left-wing critic Raymond Williams found himself a working-class boy in a grammar school classroom, and the study of literature was 'where the experience of inequality came though'.[4] As Williams there indicates, it is as the student reads a text written with another kind of reader in mind that she or he learns to position themselves as outside the group directly addressed by the work, as not specifically included.

These are the kinds of discovery in the classroom which, I believe, are at the cutting edge of progress in tolerance and understanding of diversity in higher education. Forget about the tabloid scare-headline fantasies about policing the language and erasing tradition from the canon. I travel a lot, and teach in a lot of universities here and in the United States, and I have yet to encounter one real life example of such bowdlerising or crass strait-jacketing. There *are* of course many occasions on which a teacher prefers some works over others, or encourages students to concentrate on part only of an extensive reading list. What is known as the canon (by analogy with scriptural exegesis[5]) – the long list of literary texts judged formative for our culture – has altered and continues to alter over time, depending on the tastes and special cultural concerns of the age. And in every period it has been open to literary critics to ignore 'central' works and select 'marginal' ones for study for some specified intellectual purpose, without accusations of 'policing'. For every work not attended to in this year's syllabus there is a work to which critical scrutiny is given for the first time (or given again, after a period of silence and neglect) and which enriches our understanding of our literary heritage in fresh ways.

PC is about *enlarging* our horizons. PC is about remembering that students do not all come from the same home backgrounds, and that it is not therefore educationally productive to refer familiarly to formative reading to which they did not have access. It is not difficult to find a really basic example of the way in which students can be grouped according to their pre-university reading. While I was a lecturer at Cambridge I gave a course on 'the renaissance intellectual tradition', during which I remarked that every sixteenth-century schoolchild would certainly have been familiar with the names and adventures from Greek and Roman mythology, and that an author like Shakespeare could rely on immediate recognition when he used characters like Hippolyta and Theseus (in *A Midsummer Night's Dream*), or when he had his heroine Rosalind, disguised as a boy, take the name Ganymede in *As You Like It*.[6] To illustrate the point from our contemporary experience I asked my audience of 150 or so who had been read A. A. Milne's *Winnie the Pooh* as their bedtime story as a child. Ninety per cent of that audience had cut their milk teeth on Christopher Robin. In other words, this was a nearly uniform group of children of middle-class professional people, for whom the rather difficult syntax and highly ironised, adult-orientated stories about a toy bear provide pleasurable bedtime diversion. PC in the university classroom means opening the resources of a rich and diverse cultural heritage to those traditionally excluded. It means noticing (for example) that most of the value judgements enshrined in the teaching texts used in our classrooms are those of middle-class, Oxbridge-educated men, and that this might make it hard for students not drawn from that background to respond to their arguments with that easy recognition we reward as 'ability' when grading their examinations and essays.

Critical selection is always an act of intervention, and is always open to the charge that it prejudges what the reader is allowed to think. Let's return for a moment to the two surviving versions of *Othello* with which I began. Take that speech of Emilia's in *Othello* in which she speaks up on behalf of women – a speech which is to be found in only one of the early printed texts:

> But I do think it is their husbands' faults
> If wives do fall. Say that they slack their duties
> And pour our treasures into foreign laps,
> Or else break out in peevish jealousies,
> Throwing restraint upon us; or say they strike us,
> Or scant our former having in despite –
> Why, we have galls, and though we have some grace
> Yet have we some revenge.[7]

Without this speech, the scene in which Desdemona sings the 'willow song' – the song of a lover abandoned by her beloved, who takes the blame for the breakdown in the relationship – becomes a stylised, emblematic representation of female passivity and culpability. With Emilia's assertive counterpoint the scene becomes one which struggles with female and male responsibility and its limitations and negotiations. What begins as an editorial decision – do we base our play-text on the surviving quarto or the folio text? – becomes the crux in our interpretation of the play. Is Desdemona entirely wronged, or does she succumb to the inevitable consequences of female assertiveness in choice of marriage partner? In the terms of the current debate, inclusion of

Emilia's speech is the 'politically correct' editorial decision. It makes prominent injustice against women. It offers the possibility (even in 1623) of a 'feminist' response to Othello's harsh treatment of his wife. Kiernan Ryan picks out precisely this speech for special attention in his 'New Readings' textbook on Shakespeare:

> I want to spotlight in particular that extraordinary exchange between Emilia and Desdemona in the final scene of Act IV, an exchange whose unsettling ramifications the presiding critical accounts have failed to register – not least, no doubt, because they vex the most vulnerable prejudices of an overwhelmingly male academic establishment. With Othello now possessed beyond dissuasion by murderous jealousy, on the very threshold of the catastrophe of Act V, the two women fall to talking about the rights and wrongs of adultery, and the scene closes with this trenchant, impassioned speech by Emilia on the consequences of the inequality and injustice built into marriage:
>
> > But I do think it is their husband's [sic] faults
> > If wives do fall. [. . .]
>
> This remarkable passage invites us to recognise that the true sexual tragedy is the result of Othello's imprisonment within the male version of marital jealousy and the patriarchal structure of domination and possession of which such jealousy is the direct consequence . . . The whole scene . . . offers an egalitarian female perspective on the drama.[8]

If, that is, our edition of the play has chosen to include the speech as part of Shakespeare's 'authentic' play. So here, a brush with PC in the literary lecture hall is a matter of inclusion or exclusion: it is PC to prefer the text which contains the 'oppositional' or contentious lines – the ones which allow the critic to find incipient feminism in the words of the heroine's maidservant.

We do not have to agree. Probably the most widely held misunderstanding about PC in education is that it is coercive. I do not happen to agree with Ryan about Emilia's speech. I think any feminist ought to be dismayed at the suggestion that the single speech on behalf of women is placed in the mouth of the very character who is neither listened to nor believed until after Desdemona's murder. Nevertheless, the realisation that this speech is considered appropriate in one version of this scene (but not another) as in some way highlighting or counterpointing Desdemona's passivity and resigned acceptance of the loss of her husband's affection allows us to focus our attention on the issue of gender here. It opens up discussion of how historically a wife's behaviour was perceived in relation to her husband's treatment of her (whether or not that treatment was reasonable).

In a mixed classroom such a discussion allows serious consideration of a whole range of topics triggered by 'difference' – by recognising that there are many possible positions for one as respondent to the stage action: that of the man, that of the woman; that of the Black man, that of the less advantaged woman. Once again this opening up aerates the debate. It widens the mesh which defines the shape of our critical attention, and allows glimpses of alternative points of view. Instead of locating itself in the position of the dominant culture and consigning those who do not recognise themselves there to the position of passive spectators, it operates inclusively and thickens the texture of the critical exchange by incorporating interactions and countermoves by those not accustomed to being listened to.

Political correctness in the classroom addresses just this muted (and often largely unrecognised) sense of exclusion. Insofar as it is a term which means anything (no literary critic would find it a helpful term to use themselves), it describes the teacher's commitment to making all teaching inclusive, faced with an increasingly diverse undergraduate population. When I was an undergraduate at Cambridge we women students sat respectfully through lectures in the English Faculty in which, for example, we were told that no reader could help becoming romantically entangled with the emotionally vulnerable, physically fragile, heroine of Henry James's *The Wings of the Dove*, Milly Theale – she was everyone's dream of a young woman in need of cherishing and protecting.[9] It did not cross our minds that such a reading excluded us. But it did mean that we found difficulties in following the (male) lecturer's sophisticated analysis of the novel from this particular point of view. Such criticism has quietly receded in importance in the leading critical journals (though I doubt whether it has lost its hold on a good number of classrooms). Thos who affect horror at the thought of political correctness in the university lecture hall are no longer overly exercised by the idea that lecturers in English literature might adopt critical positions available to both female and male members of their audiences – after all, well over 60 per cent of the audience in any literature department in Britain will be young women. 'PC' is an accusation only levelled at moves towards inclusiveness which are controversial and seem to go against the grain of customary thinking; once the group bidding for recognition is recognised (in this case, women in higher education in the humanities) the strategies for inclusion are no longer even noticed.

Care with inclusive language in the university, as in every other classroom, is part of the pedagogic contract to impart education to everyone who has gained access (in higher education, competitively) to that classroom. All teaching will strive to include all students, whatever their gender, race, religious preference, age or (to as large an extent as possible) ability. In a lecture on a Shakespeare comedy, early on in my time at the University of London, I gave extended attention to a passage of wordplay in which two women were contrasted as 'fair' and 'black'. The Princess of Navarre in *Love's Labours Lost* is politically and economically important, and the object of the romantic attentions of a prince. Her companion is of less elevated birth, less dynastically important, and a comparatively peripheral figure in the plot. As I explained, this is why she is referred to as 'black' – because she is of little consequence, is of minor interest, is inferior. I watched an Afro-Caribbean woman student flinch. However carefully that point of early modern language had been explained, it would have caused difficulty for a sensitive Black student. But we can take care when we explicate such points to show that we recognise the difficulty. That is political correctness.

What about the literary canon? University teachers are supposed to have removed offensive books from their reading lists and from the library shelves, 'banning' works by white male authors which purportedly enshrine opinions now labelled 'incorrect'. According to the tabloids primary school teachers have removed *Little Black Sambo* from the school library; presumably we would remove

Marlowe's *The Jew of Malta* because of its representation of the Jew as murderous, randomly destructive and generally hateful. In fact we don't remove books. F. R. Leavis thought Milton's epic poem *Paradise Lost* had damaged English versification and ought not to be studied by students; liberal teachers tend to advocate wide and diverse reading; nowadays, on diminishing grants, allowing purchase of fewer and fewer books, and publishing strategies which mean 'classics' are often out of print, the problem for the students is to get access to the requisite reading at all.

The charge that PC teachers expurgate the canon happens to be a subject close to my own heart and personal experience. In autumn 1992 the edited letters of 1950s poet Philip Larkin were published, and produced a spasm of angry debate in the press and on arts programmes like 'The Late Show'. Larkin's letters (particularly his letters to author Kingsley Amis) turned out to contain offensive remarks of a puerile kind about women, about foreigners, about Asian immigrants . . . about a whole raft of things which were customarily comfortably vilified in private in postwar Britain. Liberal critics denounced Britain's favourite poet as personally despicable (but hadn't we always known that), at the same time quickly affirming with great solemnity that the poetry was of such superlative quality that we would just have to live with the discrepancy between man and oeuvre (not for the first time, of course: what about Ezra Pound's flirtation with fascism and T. S. Eliot's anti-semitism?). Traditionalists extolled the published letters as showing us the man 'in the round and in the raw', and reaffirmed their undying commitment to the poet of the little man ('They fuck you up, your Mum and Dad'), warts and all. In the midst of what I suppose could only be called a critical row, I was asked by the *Guardian* if I would write a feature article about the Larkin *Letters*. I include some of that piece here, because the tone of what I wrote is important for what followed its publication. The article began as follows:

> The students in my University Department of English are for the most part neither Anglo-Saxon nor male. Furthermore, the Anglo-Saxons and the young men belong to a generation whose face is turned towards the new Europe, and for whom comfortable British insularity holds no romance. The publication of the *Selected Letters of Philip Larkin 1940–1985*, edited by Anthony Thwaite, has therefore landed my lecturer colleagues and myself with a problem.[10]

My starting-point, in other words, was a particular teaching problem: what are we to do when publication of 'research material' associated with a canonical author (it was taken for granted by everyone that Larkin *is* in the canon, though strictly, I think, canonicity runs out of steam somewhat earlier) reveals him to be out of tune with the attitudes, beliefs and value system of those who study him?

> Our problem concerns the place Larkin's poetry occupies at the heart of the traditional canon of English Literature. Its place, that is, within that body of works cherished by defenders of British culture as the repository of the Best of British – those sentiments and ideas which allow our culture to reflect the standards and values which the educated world considers

> universally valid. Can we continue to present the poetic writings of Larkin as self-evidently 'humane' when the student who consults the *Selected Larkin Letters* in the College Library confronts a steady stream of casual obscenity, throwaway derogatory remarks about women, and arrogant disdain for those of different skin colour or nationality?

I hastened to insist that we would *not* try to 'censor' or 'ban' the Larkin *Letters*. 'We encourage our students to "read around" their key literary texts. A significant part of their training consists in juxtaposing careful reading of the text with equally careful exploration of the life and thought of the period which produced it.' Rather, the problem with the *Letters* was precisely how clearly they revealed that the casual assumptions of insular Little Englishness are an integral part of the cultural milieu out of which a classic poem like 'Whitsun Wedding' was born:

> The *Letters* alert us to a cultural frame within which Larkin writes, one which indeed takes racism and sexism for granted as crucially a part of the British national heritage. The trouble with our encounter with the Larkin letters, in fact, is that we are not a bit surprised by them. They are part of the fabric of everyday British life. Written against a background of everyday discrimination, everyday assumptions of white British superiority, Larkin's poems, likewise, leave familiar prejudices intact. They do not engage with them, in spite of their own resolutely everyday texture and quality. The very familiarity of the poetic tone, its easy reference to what we know and love, masks its implications for those who 'don't belong'.

> The Britishness of Larkin's poetry carries a baggage of attitudes which the *Selected Letters* now make explicit.

The problem for the teacher, in other words, is: What are we to do with the realisation that a familiar author assumes *throughout his work* that the values and beliefs he and his readers subscribe to are exclusive to an Anglo-Saxon brotherhood of slightly depressed under-achievers? The solution we had reached in my Department of English, I informed *Guardian* readers, was not to 'ban' Larkin's poetry (which in any case almost every student had studied at school), but to contextualise him in a specialist second year course on 'Fifties British Poetry'. A wider frame of reference, more culturally inclusive and alert to the values of a more diverse and multicultural Britain, had inevitably, I suggested, 'edged Larkin from the centre of the margins'.

In the weeks following the publication of my piece I learned to my cost what passionate commitment to Larkin's poetry could produce in the way of values. I was deluged in letters, ranging from the indignant to the abusive, all of which accused me of 'banning' or 'censoring' Larkin, and many of which told me to 'go back where I came from' (I suppose I *am* of immigrant stock), that the government should stop wasting taxpayers' money on people like me, and (memorably) that it was because I had spent too long teaching 'wogs in the East End' that I held such warped and disgraceful views. I was genuinely astonished at the discourtesy, the intolerance, the deliberate aggression, and the absolute lack of humaneness of these letters. It was as if each of these correspondents had set out intentionally to confirm for me that if you steeped yourself in poetry of petty patriotism and celebration of low achievement, the values you learned were those of intemperate and embittered resentment.

English literature has only been taught in our universities since the end of the nineteenth century. A central justification for the study of English literature as a discipline in the arguments advanced by advocates of higher literary studies like Charles Kingsley and Matthew Arnold was that literature enshrined the most treasured values and beliefs of our culture. Close and critical reading of literature in English, they argued, was as valuable for our society as had been close and critical reading of the Greek and Latin classics (included within the universities since the early sixteenth century). The only difference between the sort of reading we do in my university (called 'PC') and that which Arnold had in mind is that the range of our attention has been broadened to include the diversity which is now definitive of British cultural life. We are no longer a homogeneously Christian, classically educated, roast-beef eating community; we are a rainbow alliance of faiths and practices. The 'common values' we all adhere to now are those that this rich mix has produced, and will go on producing. They are necessarily less 'insular' than those our forebears subscribed to when we were an isolated Anglo-Saxon island nation.

It is true that when an author ceases to answer teaching needs (as I believe Larkin has) she or he is moved to the margins of the curriculum. It is true that a growing interest on the part of our students in women's writing has led to our giving more attention to authors neglected by traditional critics: Aphra Behn was a major author as far as Voltaire was concerned, but a minor one for early twentieth-century critics of seventeenth-century literature. Charlotte Brontë was always granted a place in the canon for *Jane Eyre*, but not for *Shirley* or *Villette*; her sister Emily's *Wuthering Heights* was one of those precarious works discarded or included depending on whether 'hysterical' authors were in or out of fashion. Nowadays all these works are taught and studied. Meanwhile, Shakespeare has never (*pace* successive Tory education ministers) been dropped from *any* English literature course in this country, so far as I am aware. Yet the accusation is regularly levelled at university teachers that 'all they teach is incomprehensible language', while their copies of Shakespeare have been shredded.

I think my Larkin experience is typical. PC is a convenient bogyman for those who fear that the diversification of our community and the cultures it produces will end up dislodging them from their own position as typical of (and therefore able to speak out on behalf of) the nation. We all regret the passing of an age when we could claim a homogeneous culture, which was unmistakably shaped by Britain's international status as a world power and its prominence in world affairs. Women, perhaps, are a little more sanguine about that nostalgia for an inclusive voice, since at over 50 per cent of the population (and well over 60 per cent of those in any group studying English literature at university) they nevertheless found themselves so regularly outside that inclusive 'we', even then. Crying 'PC' is a way of putting one's fingers in one's ears and insisting that cultural change is being manipulated and policed by some sinister group. Troublingly, 'lefty' intellectuals and university teachers are in the front line of those thus accused. In the moment of panic when an individual recognises that she or he feels helpless, faced with the fragmentation of attitudes and beliefs which are the inevitable consequence of a pluralistic and open society, she or he casts around for a scapegoat. If understanding culture is the job of intellectuals and university teachers, then loss of understanding must be their fault. We might remind ourselves that in all totalitarian states intellectuals have traditionally been blamed for undermining the moral fibre of the state, for proposing a broader spectrum of values and attitudes, beyond dogma and dictat. Silencing them has historically been part of the strategy of every dictator.

What we need to do is to stop responding reactively to the PC attacks in the tabloids with equivalent outcries protesting our innocence – protesting that each and every example was invented, biasedly reported or misunderstood. Instead we need seriously to consider how profound is the national malaise about cultural identity, a specifically British education and the values appropriate to our nation at the end of the twentieth century. I am a teacher because I believe that remedying this malaise can only be achieved from the ground up – by educating successive generations of our brightest young people to take pleasure in the richness and diversity – even the strangeness – of contemporary British culture. Writing essays like this one on PC is, for me, part of the process of educating a wider public to understand what drives our urge to be inclusive in the classroom, but it is a distraction. It distracts, in the end, from the purposeful process of broadening each and every individual's grasp on the exciting cultural mix which is now Britain's real heritage.

NOTES

1 N. Sanders (ed.), *Othello*, New Cambridge edition, CUP, 1984, p.11.

2 M. R. Ridley (ed.), *Othello*, Arden edition, Methuen, 1958, p. li.

3 See, for instance, W. James and C. Harris (eds), *Inside Babylon: The Caribbean Diaspora in Britain*, Verso, 1993.

4 'Culture was the way in which the process of education, the experience of literature, and – for someone moving out of a working-class family to a higher education – inequality came through . . . This is, I think, still the most important way to follow the argument about culture, because everywhere, but very specifically in England, culture is one way in which class, the fact of major divisions between men, shows itself.' Raymond Williams, 'Culture and revolution: a comment', in T. Eagleton and B. Wicker (eds), *From Culture to Revolution*, Sheed and Ward, 1968, pp. 22–34.

5 For scriptural exegetes the 'canon' is the agreed list of sacred texts upon which interpretation is based. Interestingly, it too alters with time – some 'marginal' texts becoming more central, while others receive less attention or are discarded as 'apocryphal'.

6 Theseus, king of Athens and son of Aegeus, won Hippolyta, queen of the Amazons, for his wife when he and Hercules conquered the Amazons; Ganymede was cupbearer to Zeus (king of the Gods), with whom Zeus became infatuated, occasioning the anger of his wife, Hera.

7 *Othello* 4.3.82–9. Lines 82–99 are in the first folio text, but not in the 1622 quarto.

8 K. Ryan, *Harvester New Readings: Shakespeare*, Harvester Wheatsheaf, 1989, pp. 55–6.

9 I choose this example because Su Kappeler has beautifully used it to explicate the critical habits which have traditionally favoured gendered reading. See S. Kappeler, 'Falling in love with Milly Theale: patriarchal criticism and Henry James', *Feminist Review* 13, 1983, pp. 17–34.

10 3 December 1992.

Meera Syal

PC: GLC

I was having a fantasy about being Michael Crichton's agent. And in this fantasy, in which I am a white plump balding man in a dogtooth seersucker suit, I am pitching my client's latest blockbuster to a panel of shark-eyed studio executives. 'See, you know and I know that Michael has this gift, right? I mean, he knows what people are scared about, what their deepest bogymen are, before they know it themselves. What happens when man plays god with technology? *Jurassic Park*. What happens when you realise your biggest investors are your worst xenophobic nightmare? *Rising Sun*. But this latest cookie makes the other books look like stale apple-pie. Get this. A good-hearted, decent, family-minded executive is being sexually harassed by a superior. And no one will believe him. Yeah, I said to him. Cos forget Japs, forget Tyrannosaurus Rex, your biggest bogey person is here and it is woman. I'll wait for your first offer. Will someone validate my parking on the way out?'

Ten years ago, no studio executive would have touched Crichton's latest oeuvre, *Disclosure*, with a ten-foot pole. The bestselling book, which depicts Thomas Sanders' seemingly futile fight to bring his predatory female boss to justice, is billed as a 'breathtaking thriller that redraws the frontline in the sex war'. In the 1980s, we had *Nine To Five* with Dolly Parton and Jane Fonda bringing their sexist male boss to his knees, but like Crichton's PR says, in the 1990s, it's a whole new ballgame with constantly shifting goalposts. Hollywood more than most rolls with the tide of general public opinion. So if Hollywood feels the cry of the emasculated American white male is a safe bet, if their audience research tells them that *Disclosure* will speak not only to Brad in New York but also to Herbie in Minnesota, then we must accept that the backlash against PC does not exist only in the paranoid fantasies of a few self-referential soft left magazines, it is a reality at least in America.

But of course, here in Britain we like to imagine we are not such easy fodder for the invasion of isms to which our American cousins regularly open their borders. Psychotherapy, EST, silicone implants, capitalist evangelists, all sound American exports which only found a limited market in good old, no nonsense Britain. We like to think it is our inbred sense of irony (some might call it apathy) which prevents us from swallowing our placebos whole.

While the Americans may have embraced concepts such as positive discrimination, ethnic quota systems and leaflets on acceptable dating procedure, each airship of hope launched with the glitter and razzmatazz of a Las Vegas showman, somewhere in the background is the British voice of reason. I imagine her to be a small Yorkshirewoman in a headscarf who watches the take-off and mutters, 'Ay, very pretty. But you'd never get me up in one of those . . .'

So has PC ever really found a home here? If not the spacious mansion it inhabits in the USA, then maybe a small semi somewhere in Brent? Or Hackney? Or any other of those loony-lefty councils who spend your money sponsoring Bengali mat-weaving instead of paying for a new kidney for some innocent (white) child . . . Oh lord, it's all coming back now. The screaming tabloid headlines: 'Council Worker Sacked For Ordering Black Coffee!' 'School Dinner Lady Hanged For Spelling Samosa Wrong!' And the photos of weeping childminders removing Noddy from their shelves, the TV footage of grim-faced women with cropped hair and boiler suits snatching golliwogs from the arms of wailing babes . . . The jokes about the physically challenged, follicularly challenged, vertically challenged, usually told with great glee by the cerebrally challenged, making fun of the poncy lefties who couldn't let ordinary folk call a spade a bloody spade. Now granted, most of this press coverage is wedged in between Twenty Things You Never Knew About Parsnips and a pair of airbrushed nipples, but I know a backlash when I see one. Ergo, PC does exist here in some form, it wasn't a dream, Aunty Em. But why then are we left with all of the bile and none of the benefits? When did PC become a dirty word?

In the year 1979 BPC (before PC), things were rough. I can only describe this period from a personal point of view, as an Indian teenager growing up in the West Midlands. I was a pretty typical adolescent, beset by self-doubt and secret longings which I could never think of sharing with my parents. While I beavered away at 'sensible' O-level subjects, I longed to be an actress. Unfortunately, the only role models I had, the only visible Asian women in the media, were a barely literate woman in a sari in the sitcom, 'Mind Your Language', who spent most of her limited screen time saying 'Golly gosh' and knitting bootees in unspeakably lurid colours, and a young beautiful presenter on a kids' show called 'Junior Show-time'. Ayesha Raif's job was to introduce various precocious child performers in a stunning double act with a puppet called Fred the Dog. No matter that Fred inevitably got the best lines, Ayesha was every Asian girl's heroine; that to us was success, 20 minutes of airtime with your hand up a dog's backside. Of course, we'd never heard phrases such as 'positive role models', but even at that age, this feeling of not-belonging was merely reinforced by the minimal and overwhelmingly negative depiction of us, *British* Asians, in the media.

And just to rub salt into this hidden wound, the National Front seemed to be everywhere. They campaigned on TV, they marched down the end of my street, the very media which kept us out welcomed them in under the banner of free speech. They gained a public profile that made me wish I was invisible.

And then, something happened in Southall. Up until then, Southall was merely the far-flung West London suburb my parents dragged me to for a quick fix of 'home'; a little India, our patch where you could stock up on your shopping and eat food that tasted of smoky coffee houses back in Delhi. But watching the news footage of Asian youth breaking down police barriers, Indian grannies throwing chilli powder in police dogs' eyes, and the shocked, disbelieving faces of the NF members who had thought marching through this town over the heads of a few passive Pakis would be a doddle, I knew for the first time I was not alone and I did belong. A whole new generation had sprung up, nurtured in the hard soil of urban Britain and not in the soft loam of their parents' Punjab, who burned with the fury of the dispossessed that had at that point found a means of expression only in physical violence. They needed a voice that was something beyond just shouting in the streets. They needed access to the institutions, they needed a whole new vocabulary to argue their case eloquently and they now had the ear and the good will of more than a few powerful white liberals who were ashamed of what Britain was becoming. In amongst all the derision that the PC movement is now attracting, it's important to remember the sense of anger and injustice from which it sprang. In 1979, we never imagined that 15 years later, this struggle would be reduced to an argument about not calling your Uncle Ernie a slaphead. But then again, in the same year some people were celebrating the election of a certain M. Thatcher, convinced that a woman in high office was a step forward for everyone who cared about equality.

The changes in attitude caused by Southall and other uprisings during the next few years in Moss Side, Toxteth, Handsworth were at first subtle, almost unnoticeable, certainly in my part of the world. The first indication I had of a growing consciousness was noticing the blurb that began appearing at the foot of some situations vacant:

'Marleys Ballbearings is an Equal Opportunities Employer'. (This in a local paper which a year earlier had invited an NF council candidate to write an opinion column.) Then the appearance of certain news items: 'Mayor Attends Local Diwali Celebrations', 'Council Funds Afro-Caribbean Writers' Group', 'Schoolchildren Celebrate Eid in Style!' My mother, who is a primary school teacher, came home with a load of books in which chatty rainbow-coloured children replaced the stuffy, passive meanderings of Janet and John. Always ahead of the times, my mum, she had been questioned by the headmistress five years earlier when she refused to read *Noddy goes to Africa* to her four-year-olds. 'Awful dialogue,' she recalled. 'Noddy threatening to send some poor naughty child to Africa where the savages have no manners. And now they want me to bring a sari for the dressing-up box in the Wendy house . . .'

But she was not the only one of our acquaintances being similarly pursued for their ethnic contribution to various institutions. Uncles and aunties of mine who for years had been toiling away in schools, council offices, social work, who with the hardened experience of first-generation immigrants had come to accept they would have to work twice as hard to stay abreast of their white counterparts, were now being actively encouraged to progress. You cannot imagine what an ironic turnaround this was for them, the very cultural differences they had learned to hide for the sake of 'integration' into their workplaces (integration in the early 1970s meant fitting in, in order to be accepted) were now being promoted and sometimes even celebrated by their employers. It would be easy to look back on this period as some kind of council-funded nirvana, but no one felt surprised, or even grateful.

Instead, the overwhelming feeling was one of relief. All these people had children and worried desperately about their futures; they knew their kids' knowledge of the Motherland would only ever be second hand, they wondered whether their efforts to pass on their language, religion and customs to their children could survive the onslaught of society's pressures to conform. And now, suddenly, Britain was finally admitting that it was indeed a multiracial community. They did not see this as an act of charity but as one of common sense.

So even in our tiny Midland backwater, the ripples of change were rocking various institutional boats; but I wanted to be where the big stone throwing was going on. And the person lobbing the heaviest boulders was a small mustachioed man who had a soft spot for newts. Ken Livingstone was the nearest thing we had to a folk hero when I reached Manchester University in the mid-1980s. Fellow students from London would come back from a weekend visit and we'd gather round them in the coffee bar to hear the latest instalment of the revitalisation of our capital. It seemed to me that London was one big party, every weekend marked with several huge free outdoor events, live music, performance artists, multicultural *melas*, all with crèche facilities and heavily subsidised buses and tubes to get you safely home. There was talk of London feeling more like a European city, it had a nightlife, a café society, a sense of adventure and movement, it had a current running through it as swift and powerful as the River Thames. More importantly, it was the first time that an elected council was making very public and legislative steps to tackle racism and inequality; for us, it was the beginning, when the words were made flesh, and the words were equal opportunity. For my generation, PC with all its connotations of giving the underdog a voice and status was represented most visibly by the policies of the GLC.

So when I finally arrived in London with bags and baggage, ready to take the theatre world by storm, it didn't take me long to make friends. After every performance, in every pub or coffee bar I visited, I stumbled upon the kind of kindred spirits I had prayed for years to meet back in Walsall. Yes, many of them were Asian or Black, many were white, but all of them came from the generation who had watched the footage from Southall and vowed that things must change. They had found their natural home in London, they were setting up race awareness units, funding new Black writing, doing translation work in courts, monitoring housing allocations, running domestic violence units, changing, so they thought, the course of history.

Looking back on that description, it reads like a cast list for a sketch on 'Spitting Image'. Did anyone I know really spend hours arguing semantics, chairman versus chairperson, fireman versus firefighter? I can't honestly recall. What I do remember was a distinct lack of irony about the whole of the PC movement of which these people, I suppose, were the footsoldiers. The commitment was genuine, anti-racist policy and positive discrimination were not only working, they were keeping these workers in work. Hell, PC was paying my bills too, in a roundabout sort of way, because as an Asian woman I could not have chosen a better time to become an actress. Writers, as always, were at the forefront of this debate and a rash of new plays hit the theatres, all clamouring to give this new generation of angry young men and women their voice. Dramatically speaking, this was an eminently sensible move. What could the middle-class white male shout about now, being in PC terms the lowest, most insignificant member of the pecking order? John Osborne's kitchen sink ranters had moved into the suburbs and spent their days writing moaning letters to *The Times*, the most dynamic and energetic stories were coming from us, us on the so-called margins of society. We had a cause, conflict is the basis of good drama, I got offered lots of work. Sorted.

It was somewhere around my second year in the business, after a week of auditions in which I'd been asked to play two victims of arranged marriage, three downtrodden shopkeepers' wives, four harassed NHS doctors and a woman in an ad for a government retraining scheme, that the word tokenism began to flutter round my head. At first it seemed ungrateful to complain, especially when I got talking to the older Asian actors I knew who reminded me that ten years earlier maybe one part a year would come up for someone with a non-white face. I was canny enough to realise that being an Asian female loaded me with Brownie points, certainly enough to get a foot in the door. But I hoped, I prayed, that it would be my abilities rather than my colour which pushed it open and led me into other bigger, better rooms. But I resented this feeling of suspicion, this niggling whisper that 'you only got the job because you are Asian', and this was steadily being compounded by the quality of the parts I was being offered. I knew most of the roles I was going up for were written with the noblest intentions, by white writers wanting to understand, wanting to redress our previous invisibility. But frankly, playing eternally noble, hard-done-by victims is somewhat limiting after a while; rounded characters, real people have layers, make mistakes, and what white writer in this atmosphere was going to have the courage to do that? And that, dear reader, is exactly why I started writing.

I did not see this as biting the hand that was feeding me, more like giving it a gentle lick. If PC was about giving minorities a voice, then surely it was logical we should be speaking for ourselves instead of becoming mouthpieces to express white liberal guilt. I had already co-written a one-woman comedy show, *One Of Us*, about a young Asian girl who leaves home to become an actress (did loads of research on that one), which I had performed as a student in my final year at university and which suddenly took off like a rocket, winning prizes at the National Student Drama festival and the Edinburgh Fringe, and was eventually televised where a director spotted me and offered me my first job at the Royal Court complete with equity card. Fairytale, huh? But there were two good reasons why this show attracted critical and popular attention; one was the time – nothing more PC than a runaway Asian Brummie – and the other was that it was funny. The biggest pull was that it showed that Asian women, yes, we doe-eyed maidens in saris walking five paces behind our husbands, could be rude, irreverent and ironic.

The biggest, maybe the only advantage in being a stereotype is that you have the ability to continually surprise, to upturn audience expectation and glimpse the truth behind the cliché. I needed an antidote to all this earnestness, I wanted people to listen not because they felt they ought to, but because they wanted to. I didn't want to be on a stage haranguing people about my misery, I wanted to burst on to it in a blaze of light and colour to celebrate my differences and mock those who saw these differences as a handicap. Freud described a joke as a pleasure-bribe; we take the most frightening taboos – sex, death, outsiders – wrap them up in a funny line to make them palatable and the sharp intake of breath will bubble out as a laugh. PC had forced many people to face their deepest, most buried prejudices and so it was no surprise that the comedy circuit was thriving and I found my next niche.

Coincidentally, many of the 'alternative comedians' as they are now known had passed through my university drama department a few years before me. Ben Elton, Rik Mayall, Ade Edmonson were all strutting their stuff while I was making my first tentative steps as an actress/writer. All the old victims of punchlines, the mothers-in-law, Pakistanis, tarty women, gays, were being replaced with a vengeance with new targets: Mrs T, the police, anyone with a mobile phone. Every former sacred cow was being dragged mooing to the comedy abattoir, Bernard Manning's opening gag was rewritten to read, 'A Pakistani, an Irishman and a Gay walked into a pub and had a nice long chat . . .' I began to get writing commissions, first as a jobbing writer on other people's series, then a short film, a longer film for BBC 2 and finally, a feature film, a comedy, *Bhaji On the Beach*, charting the fortunes of a group of Asian women on a day trip to Blackpool. Okay, maybe I'd got in by hanging on to the coat tails of PC, I'd arrived in an atmosphere where the commissioning powers were now willing to listen, but I knew I had to grab this opportunity to create my own work if I wanted to play satisfying, truthful roles.

Most importantly, as an actress and a writer, I felt I finally had the go ahead to explore with honesty and without fear the issues affecting my particular, unique generation. In ten years, we had moved from walk-on artists to major players. In 'My Sister Wife', the BBC 2 film I wrote and acted in, all four major characters were Asian. One scene which many people seem to remember is when Sabia, an elderly Asian woman, is handing round starters to guests at her son's party. As she speaks to a white guest in Punjabi, subtitles telling us what she's really saying appear on the screen: 'I don't have to do this, you know. We have an English maid. Now you are serving us, good one, eh?' The guest thinks she's commenting on the food and takes a second helping, assuming she's the cook. Sabia upturned every expectation in this brief exchange; she not only showed an ironic awareness of her situation, she also showed how revenge for the inequalities of the past can make racists of us all.

Interestingly, 'My Sister Wife', about a westernised Pakistani woman, Farah, who agrees to become the second wife of a Pakistani man with whom she has fallen obsessively in love, was more or less ignored by the liberal white press. I could see why; it did not fit into the easy anti-racist categories that had been set up. It wasn't about helpless Asians being firebombed in their council flats (though God knows, enough of it was going on), and it did not divide its cast into brown goodies and white baddies. Rather, it took a polygamous set up in a wealthy family as a metaphor for the painful adaptation processes facing women of my generation.

To me, this was artistic freedom, that I could turn inwards and look at the struggles within my community, within the individual, rather than always examining how the host society saw and treated us. Of course, the two are inextricably linked: how you are seen forces you to question what and where you are. But I felt as if PC was now dividing itself into two separate stages. The first stage, in which racism was dragged into the open and rightly vilified, lent itself to angry, anti-white drama, an outpouring of our frustrations and white sympathy. The second, more interesting stage was beginning now the anger was abating, in which we could now explore deeper issues of identity with confidence and, we hope, humour. This no longer felt like favouritism. It felt like growing up.

It took me about five years to write *Bhaji*, in between other rent-paying writing and acting jobs, and from the window of my study over that period I saw the death of PC as it happened, symbolised by the changing fortunes of my new neighbours, the Yuppies. When I first moved into my Clapham flat, it was a predominantly 'family' street, some lone old people who had lived there for years and one or two singles like myself glad to have snapped up the few houses being converted into flats. I swear it seemed to happen overnight, the scaffolding suddenly springing up on every other building, Golf GTI's clogging the narrow road, chippies being replaced by wine bars and lots of Sunday softball matches on the nearby common. Suddenly money was the new equaliser; if Kevin from a comprehensive school in Essex could clear 50K on the futures market, then who was going to listen to a few moaning minnies bleating on about discrimination? The shift in public tolerance was subtle but gradual and constant. At first the tone was affectionate mockery, 'Ken Gives Money To Lesbian Darts Team'; two favourite cartoon characters appeared in newspapers, the Hooray Hooligan, pissed, mobile phone in hand, the vegetarian, woolly cardigan do-gooder, both amply representing the two forces fighting for the capital. Then the Tory government began to get extremely nervous about how popular this Livingstone chappie seemed to be. County Hall is just across the Thames from the Houses of Parliament, and it must have seemed to the Tories that after each policy they pushed through, the sound of hooting and loud raspberries would come drifting across the water. After all, Greater London had its own council and its own very definite and separate agenda, anti-racism and equal opportunity policies being two of its cornerstones. So naturally, the GLC had to go.

The concerted press campaign to get rid of the GLC, led by London's only evening paper, was truly awesome in its ferocity. Soon after, the bubble of easy money burst. Shares plunged, inflation rocketed, the builders on my road went home and my next door neighbour became the first victim of a repossession I had ever met. Sadly, he wasn't the last either. The 'alternative' comics who a few years earlier had been hailed as social satirists now became the objects of satire, a puppet of Ben Elton appearing on 'Spitting Image', and contemporaries of Bernard Manning such as Frankie Howerd and Bruce Forsyth were welcomed back with loving arms as true, unappreciated geniuses. The boom was over and during it a whole new underclass had gradually been created, quite logical when you know that if somebody's making loadsamoney, some other poor bugger is going without. For the average citizen landed with a crippling mortgage that five years earlier had seemed manageable, accosted on the street by beggars (beggars in London!), stepping over people sleeping in the doorway of Debenhams, there was no distinction between victim and victimiser any more. So the Blacks had it bad, so gays felt persecuted, so who gave a toss when we were all deep in doo doo?

The huge firework display over the Thames marked the end of the GLC and, for many of my friends, not only the end of an era but the end of their official employment. Those that had assumed they could take their skills elsewhere by moving sideways into other government bodies were cruelly disappointed, as one by one, various London councils went into local elections red and came out blue or occasionally went orange. One of my friends was due to start a new job with Ealing Council's Women's Unit the day before local elections; the day after, the Tories got in and disbanded the whole department. This became a familiar pattern: whole departments, initiatives which had taken years to set up and run successfully were dismembered in this atmosphere of hysteria. No one wanted to have the stigma hanging over them of pandering to any minority group, now that the formerly silent majority had spoken; Uncle Ken was now Red Ken, woolly liberals wasting money on wogs and queers had got us into this mess. Hadn't they?

Despite all the setbacks of that period, *Bhaji on the Beach* actually got made. Covering nearly every 'minority' issue going – Asian women, violence against women, Black/Asian relationships, neglected housewives – it came out in 1994 to, thankfully, much critical acclaim and, inevitably, some hard-hitting criticism. There were the sniffy reviews in some right-wing tabloids, an-ethnic-hotch-potch, only-for-the-converted kind of reviews (aah, how soon they forget!). There were the liberal broadsheet reviews, important-issues, surprisingly-funny-film kind of reviews. And there were those who felt the film should not have been made at all, but I can't tell you who they were exactly, only that they were male, probably Asian, bloody angry, and rang me up to abuse me for showing our community in such a negative light. 'How dare you show our women doing such things? Talking about sex and what's worse, doing it before marriage? Showing them as frustrated when we are fighting to hold on to our culture? Painting our men as violent when the real violence is against us by white people?' Déja vu is not an adequate term for what I felt when Mr Angry of Luton began haranguing me about positive images, something about grandmothers and egg-sucking came to mind, but how can I be flippant when I understand his point of view? The film does raise contentious issues which we all known are happening, but does so with laughter; the film is overwhelmingly a comedy. There are certainly scenes which do show white racism, violent, upsetting scenes, but there are others which also show brown/Black racism and how futile and divisive this is . . .

I could go on but this is the bugger: whatever I wrote would be taken as representative because there is so little else to compare it with. If *Bhaji* was one of four films a year depicting the lives of Asian women, it would be one more story layering an incredibly complex social group. But as it stands, it is the first British feature film written and directed by Asian women. We knew that everybody would be watching. And just as the hapless Ayesha Raif with her puppet dog failed to represent all my hopes and dreams, so *Bhaji* could not possibly attempt to speak for every Asian man or woman who went to see it. Writers deal with the particular. I based many of the characters on women I know since one cannot write in generalisations and expect those characters to breathe. But it is a sad, perilous equation that every writer has to try and solve: the less we have, the more we expect our writers to redress the balance. Furthermore, the timing is unfortunate; we are somewhat under siege, we no longer have the protective umbrella of PC where we can shout 'Not fair' and be heard, anyone is fair game, and maybe trying to have an honest dialogue about what is happening within our community while it is being attacked from outside is foolish. But what are the alternatives? Writing the safe characters that offend no one and say nothing? Or, in this atmosphere of fear, is the real alternative silence? PC gave me and others like me the space to have this dialogue. God help us if the backlash against it takes that space away.

Christopher Hitchens

THE FRAYING OF AMERICA: A Review of *Culture of Complaint*, Robert Hughes

Times have changed
And we've often rewound the clock
Since the Puritans got a shock
When they landed on Plymouth Rock.
If today
Any shock they should try to stem,

'Stead of landing on Plymouth Rock,
Plymouth Rock would land on them.

Cole Porter, *Anything Goes*, 1934

'We didn't land on Plymouth Rock. Plymouth Rock landed on us!'

Malcolm in Spike Lee's *X*, 1992

In the 1960s, while exiled in Algeria from the intensifying ruthlessness of the apartheid state, the leaders of the 'black consciousness' Pan African Congress sent a letter to Evelyn Waugh. They had, they told him solemnly, read his novel *Black Mischief*. They wished to know where he had found the name 'Azania', given in the book to a hellhole of corrupt *negritude* in what Waugh would never have called the third world. And why did they wish to know? They desired a name for the future liberated South Africa, and this had struck them as a most apt and euphonious one. Waugh wrote back from his country house informing the PAC curtly (and as it happens, erroneously) that Azania was a derivation of an old Hellenistic name for a mythical African slave kingdom. As a result of this bizarre correspondence, while the multiracial and leftist ANC continued to call South Africa 'South Africa' as a matter of internationalist principle, the name 'Azania' appears on Steven Biko's tombstone and in less lapidary form in the acronyms of separatist and tribalist groups like AZAPO, who are swift to denounce 'sell-outs' like Nelson Mandela for borrowing the colonial terminology of the oppressor.

There ought to be neither shame nor surprise in the fact that macho Malcolm X – who wouldn't even own to a

'Eurocentric' name – annexed a good line from the white homosexual lyricist who composed *You're the Top*, or that African outcasts had to apply for the name of their country to the disdainful author of *Scoop*.There will always *be* mutual linguistic and cultural exchange, just as there will always *be* some kind of canon. These are reasons among many for considering the enterprise of discrete ethnic discourses and separatist canons to be doomed as well as silly. It is futile to expect, let alone to wish, that only slaves write about slavery, only women about rape, only Jews about the *Shoah*. And it will always be particularly pointless and perhaps sinister to expect or demand this in America.

The American demotic language is a pungent blend of everything from the Black pulpit to the Yiddish shrug, from the official emancipatory documents written by English slavers and gentleman-farmers to the mix of Cajun, Spanish, Calabrian and Gaelic. Who does not say, or get, '*Vaya con dios*', 'donnybrook', '*omertà*', 'For he's a jolly good fellow', 'Jacob's ladder', or 'What's not to like?' And those are only the clichés. The whole tendency of American speech and usage has been, often to the shock of fastidious European travellers, one of pith and directness. The midwestern farmer, the Harlem preacher, the blue-collar barman (I have, for obvious reasons, exempted the Manhattan cabbie) are all rightly famous, far beyond these shores, for wanting you to get the point with a minimum of delay. And 'demotic', here, has a definite relation to 'democratic'.

However, and largely for reasons of status-yearning and insecurity, there has always been an opposing tendency. All languages and cultures have a version of this, but there may be a specifically American need to take refuge in euphemism and insipid gentility. 'Will he know what this is in regards to?' trills the half-educated and half-paid secretary when you telephone the pseudoposh publishing executive. 'Sir, that's not our policy,' says an easily fired minder in some store that won't keep its word. 'Inappropriate' is bad. 'Comfortable with' is good. 'Insensitive' is the term used by the sort of people prone to announce that they themselves 'feel badly'. While of course, American bureaucratic and military coinages – 'downsizing', 'collateral damage', 'interdict' – are justly notorious on a world scale for their crude muffling of moral consequence and their subordination to the ends of power.

Robert Hughes has the distinction of being one of the few contemporary writers with no brow problem. He is a self-educated generalist, able to write for experts and for the laity. It probably helps that he is from Australia; a nation whose origins he evoked so feelingly in *The Fatal Shore*. He makes the best use, by which I mean popular rather than vulgar, of that country's tradition of blunt speech. For him, the human tongue is more of an organ than it is a tissue or a muscle, and he flinches instinctively from what the French call *langue du bois* – the infliction of jargon and dogma. He is the revenge upon the Philistines; a man who can mix it up in saloons and horse fairs as well as in salons and ateliers, and who can be elevated without condescension. If large numbers of Americans are willing to queue that extra half-hour to see an exposition of Goya or an evocation of the lost symbiosis of Andalusia, it is partly due to Hughes's careful, witty, but not too-popular essays and presentations in, of all places, *Time* magazine.

Magnetised towards America by the breadth and liberty and candour of its culture, Hughes has something of the zeal of the immigrant. Seeing American mores and language being encased in a cocoon spun from blather and drool, he has sprung forward to wake the sleeper before the threads can congeal into a carapace. The 'recovery' movement with its alarming humourless narcissism; the 'national security' babble of the state; the Balkanisation of the academy; the prohibitionist and 'family values' crowd who watch too much television – he lays about them all, and sees that they are all aspects of the same enervating self-pity and solipsism.

He is at pains to separate himself from Senator Jesse Helms, whose redoubt in North Carolina is the last bastion of the old Confederacy and whose racist and populist appeal has recently taken the form of a crusade for family values and against 'obscenity'. You could summarise Jesse Helms by saying that he would burn books but would forbid other people to burn flags. Hughes is one of the few to have noticed the embarrassing political correctness of Senator Helms's recent bill, which sought to exploit the row over Robert Mapplethorpe's graphically homosexual photography. Article Three of Helms's Philistine legislative proposal sought to impose a ban on: 'Material which denigrates, debases or reviles a person, group or class of citizens on the basis of race, sex, creed, handicap, age or national origin.' Here is Helms annexing the discourse of political correctness. But at whose expense is such an irony: the irony of the equal-opportunity bigot?

It occurs to me that Hughes's deftly made point may not have an irony at all. In other words, that there are those in the 'empowerment community' who mean business about regulating speech and expression. Let us just pause and shake ourselves for a second while the implications percolate. *For the first time in American history, those who call for an extension of rights are also calling for an abridgement of speech.*

I believe that I am right about this. The Constitution, which is elastic to infinitude about potential expansion of rights (as well it might be, given its inborn constraints against the propertyless, against women, and most shamefully against the descendants of African slavery), is also adamant about free speech and assembly and about the wrongness of an established faith. Thus, every great battle for the extension of liberty on this continent has had, in the last resort of the Constitution, the law on its side. And most if not all such contests have necessitated a parallel battle for the principle of free speech and assembly. Thus the struggle against slavery was in large part a struggle for the right to challenge calcified statutes about teaching and literacy (Charles Dickens wrote memorably that in many American cities it was more dangerous to teach a Black man to read than it was to burn him alive). Likewise the later war over segregation took the form of a fight for free assembly and the right to demonstrate and publish. In the case of labour organising, any drive against the open shop or the company town had to begin with a punch-up over the right to leaflet or to publish a newspaper. The same applies to the resistance to imperialist war and to the advocacy of the rights of women. The American Civil Liberties Union came into being because free speech was an inseparable aspect of all 'rights' disputes. And nearer to our own time, the great challenge to imperial authority on all matters had its origins in something called quite simply 'The Free Speech Movement'.

Suddenly, though, and as if to prove that no question is ever finally decided, one finds oneself in arguments over first principles. Groups that at least affirm the rhetoric and traditions of civil rights are openly saying that free expression is not a value in itself, but a contingent and relative thing. Rather than cite a plethora of examples, I would invite readers to confirm this from their own experience, in the confidence that they will be able to do so. My own chosen instance, and the one that decided me on this, was the imposition of a 'speech code' at the University of Madison in Wisconsin – a campus with a highly evolved liberal and radical tradition. The code, which took upon itself the task of deciding what was and was not 'offensive', was promulgated by Donna Shalala (now a trusted member of Clinton's cabinet) during her tenure as principal. The definition of the permissible was so arbitrary and so oppressive that it did not survive a court challenge to its constitutionality from the American Civil Liberties Union. But it became clear that university bureaucracies found it useful to annex the moral authority of victimology as an additional means of control. To hear the grammar of the 1960s liberation movement being bastardised in this way was a lesson that I decided not to be taught twice. And this is the importance of the Hughes book. Never mind that he balances each story of some 'politically correct' atrocity with an example of bluenose McCarthyite zeal, the fact is that we need no instruction in the crimes of the old-style nativist and prohibitionist censors. The pressing matter is the defence of free thinking from its false friends, not its traditional enemies. This is a case where what remains of the left has yet to find what remains of its voice.

Perhaps one should say a brief word in defence of the PC ethos. In an oblique way, it is a compliment to pluralism in the most diverse society on earth: a recognition of the multinational society and a challenge to the hegemony of the WASP ruling class. It also contains a sort of Utopianism; a touching if authoritarian belief that behaviour and expression, if properly conditioned, will actually lead to purer thoughts.

But these moralistic, idealistic constructs are in danger of metamorphosing into their opposites, if indeed they have not done so already. It is precisely because America is so 'diverse' that it is mistaken to make so much of the distinctions. Freud wrote a much-too-brief essay entitled 'The Narcissism of the Small Difference', which showed how people could be induced to quarrel more and more about less and less. The real tendency of PC is not to inculcate respect for the marvellous variety of humanity but to reduce each group into subgroups and finally to atoms, so that everyone is on their guard against everyone else.

Look at an innocuous example. The movement to ease the lives of the disabled was a classic instance of reformism at its most generous. How did we ever tolerate elevators without Braille panels; public buildings without access ramps? The general consciousness of the majority, respecting the existence of a large minority, was enhanced and nobody was the loser. Indeed, those of us who had to deal with pushchairs got a free ride as a result, with pavements and stairways made easier for all. And some thoughtless metaphors underwent reconsideration. (Because of an adored friend with chronic MS, I myself stopped employing that *New Left Review* perennial 'sclerotic' to describe petrified institutions like the British monarchy.) So far, so good. But suppose that a quadriplegic now goes to law, demanding to be allowed a job as a firefighter or on a construction site and demanding furthermore to be referred to as 'differently abled'? At once, the argument ceases to be about society and obligation. The first thing that happens is that the newly generous perceptions of the majority start to dry up. The second thing is that someone writes a paper saying that a specific issue of Cherokee lesbian paraplegics remains to be addressed. Out of the window goes all thought of solidarity, fraternity and the common good.

Hughes rightly describes this aspect of PC as a species of 'linguistic Lourdes', where the halt and the lame are expected to feel cured when addressed as 'challenged', and where bigots are reformed by going gay-bashing instead of fag-bashing. It doesn't take long, either, for the new euphemism to become the most recent insult – which is why 'queer' went full circle so fast. And would I have dropped 'sclerotic' if I had been coerced into doing so?

If a backlash does arrive, we can be sure that it will, like the Helms amendment, cloak itself in the language of victimhood. A foretaste, surely, was provided by the disgrace of the Hill–Thomas hearings, where objective deliberation was made impossible by competing claims of racism and sexism, both of them adroitly manipulated by the right. George Bush was a good little quota merchant and bean counter, as indeed Bill Clinton is turning out to be. The paltry political skill lies in doing enough bean counting to appease various sectors, while running against bean counting as such. It only takes an average machine politician a day or so to grasp this Tammany principle and to find the words with which to dignify it.

For me, there are two symbolic figures in this swirl of confusion about proper speech, 'sensitive' teaching and infinite sub-categorisation. The two are Lenny Bruce and Salman Rushdie. Bruce was a genuinely subversive (we might now say 'transgressive') comedian, for whom the whole point of humour was that it gambled with the unsayable. As it happened, he used words that were deemed bigoted or obscene in order to demystify them. An act like his is hard to imagine today, when 'comedy' oscillates between the bland, the apologetic and the defiantly nasty.

In the case of Salman Rushdie, a genuinely multicultural figure whose work and life are a synthesis of peoples and languages and histories, it has been fascinating to hear the excuses and evasions. As soon as it could be claimed that the feelings of a great religion had been in some way 'hurt', the euphemisms began to multiply. Hughes is rightly scornful of the cowardly silence of the American academy, which took refuge in half-baked talk about cultural relativism and the dangers of a Eurocentric view, not of Islam only, but of free speech as an 'abstract' principle. This high-toned temporising just chanced to dovetail nicely with the less scrupulous Western state policy of disowning Rushdie the better to resume trading arms with Iran. Those who wished to be 'non-judgemental' had in fact made a very subjective judgement, which happened to set a low value on the Enlightenment.

In the Rushdie case, also, the right abandoned its claim to be the defender of what might be called traditional values, such as free expression and opposition to theocratic tyranny. In the figure of the persecuted author, the neo-conservative intellectuals like Norman Podhoretz or Hilton Kramer could see only a secular subversive leftist ingrate. In the great contemporary test of the willingness to uphold literary and scholarly independence, they did not so much run away as actually display some sympathy for the other side.

This is why I believe that the left is missing an immense

opportunity in the PC war. It has surely become clear by now that tendencies claiming descent from first principles – first principles such as anti-racism and the equality of the sexes – have not 'gone too far' but have become something else. An urgent task, as we used to say, now confronts us. The threads of a real cultural critique have been torn apart by every species of sectarian. The 'Me decade' has become a sort of 'Me millennium', with every tribe and faction awarding primacy to its own cause. The study of history and society and literature is being atomised and turned into something arid and pointless, a mere clinic for competing resentments.

I remember feeling an uneasy premonition when, in the period of defeat and demoralisation that followed the 1960s, it was decided that the left could be revived with the assertion that 'the personal is political'. The consequences of that rather dubious claim are now all around us, except that personality has deposed politics altogether. There is, obviously, an overdue and justified impatience with the axiomatic identification of 'culture' as 'Western', and with all the implied corollaries of that. But this impatience is being frittered away and demoralised by ghettoisation and by the setting up of separate reservations. The whole of New York University has been convulsed recently by an argument over the tenure of a professor, Leonard Jeffries, who is surely entitled to his First Amendment free speech rights but who teaches garbage about the supposed ethnological differences between 'ice people' and 'sun people': Farrakhanism with a pseudo-academic veneer. Set against this the great work of Basil Davidson, in *The Black Man's Burden* and in a shelf of other scholarship, on the authentic and untaught history of Africa. We have immutable values too, and we need to defend them against the Yahoos, against the ivory tower trimmers and against those who will exploit the politics of PC to reinforce a pseudo-consensus that is paradoxically based on divide and rule. Robert Hughes shows that there is life still in the Renaissance concept of humanist education. He reminds me, also, that, like him, I didn't come all the way to America in order to watch what I say.

Lisa Appignanesi

LIBERTÉ, ÉGALITÉ AND *FRATERNITÉ*: PC AND THE FRENCH

I am sitting at a vast dinner table in a grand if somewhat ghostly apartment opposite the Elysée Palace. Myriad candles flicker over heavy silver. Voices are raised in animation, above them all the unstoppable Simone de Beauvoir-like rat-tat-tat-tat of the high-ranking academic opposite me. The recent round of GATT talks is nearing its end and the burden of La France, its republican role and unique heritage, its 330 cheeses, loom large in her discourse, as in everyone else's. Our host, who is also our chef, emerges from the kitchen – where he has been for some time – with dishes which are at once subtle and sumptuous. His wife tells me that he does all the cooking.

I seize at this smallest of threads, tug at it and urge the conversation on to the question I have asked of all and sundry during this first of my twelve months in France. What, if anything, do the French understand by political correctness and does it exist in France? There is a momentary hush round the table broken at last by a loud guffaw from the diplomat to my right. 'Political correctness,' he announces, 'is as French as cheddar cheese wrapped in plastic.'

In the subsequent months everything I have seen and heard here has corroborated this pronouncement. Examples are rife. The media regularly talks of '*l'homme*' – man – to include everyone and feel no need for any digression into man and woman. Eric Orsenna, one of France's leading novelists who worked for years as a close adviser to President Mitterand, repeatedly and blithely refers to himself as Mitterand's '*nègre*' – a word meaning both 'ghostwriter' and 'nigger'. Supermarkets display those chocolate-covered marshmallow biscuits that children adore under the label, '*Tête de nègre*' – negro's head. A male radio presenter as part of his early morning New Year's banter happily enumerates inevitably broken resolutions: 'not to smoke . . . so much, not to drink . . . so much, not to seduce . . . so much'.

At the end of 1993 *Le Nouvel Observateur*, a leading weekly, carried a cover with a headline which read 'Ideas in 1993'. Under it, were 18 photographs of intellectuals: amongst them not a single woman or 'Black' (which, given

France's ethnic composition, is most likely to be a North African, that is a Maghrebian). No one shudders. When I ask friends, 'Couldn't the *Nouvel Obs* have found even a single woman or person of colour for its round-up?' and mention a few eminent candidates, they look at me in surprise. The thought of criticising the magazine's choice on gender or racial lines has not occurred to anyone – not only men, but women, too. A similar all-male (though not always all-white) line-up regularly occurs in television panels or conferences. Only Americans or Brits seem to notice and the French, when queried, first look blank and then are quick to say that here such things are done on merit, not by quota.

In the entire programme of the famous Ecole des Hautes Etudes en Sciences Sociales, a graduate school which includes amongst its professorial luminaries Jacques Derrida and Milan Kundera, only two out of some four hundred courses have anything specifically to do with gender – though approximately one quarter of the teaching staff is female. One is a course on the anthropology and sociology of the sexes; another on the construction of social identity, which focuses on questions of both sex and race in processes of domination and exclusion. This is not to say that gender or particularly ethnicity are not discussed in other courses, but their discussion forms a part of other issues – the problems of the city, nationalism, and so on. Bookshops follow suit, devoid of sections called Women's Studies or Gay Studies.

The few miles of water I have crossed have taken me to a very different place – and not only in terms of linguistic or media or educational refinements. This is not the country of the shuddering liberal conscience or sensitive puritan guilts. Policing here, it seems, is left to the police

– and neither internalised, nor taken on board by self-designated representatives of the greater good.

Nowhere is this clearer than in the sexual domain. What on American campuses would risk instant charges of ocular harassment is a thoroughly acceptable and minute by minute occurrence. Step out into the street or into the metro and male eyes in any colour face assess you – tickle, tease, challenge, undress and pass on to the next woman. No one seems to mind. Indeed everyone, young and old, seems to dress for the part. And I must say I grow desensitised, forget thoughts of a new category of metro-rape (we all sit and stand so *very* close together), am quite happy to read my ageing attractiveness from chance passers-by.

Nor is the traffic one way. Visiting men friends confide in me that they love the brazenness of women's eyes on them, don't quite know if they're meant to pursue the challenge or whether it's just part of the excitement of the streets. This is the land of the spectacle in which one is also a participant: the country of the gaze.

When I ask people why it is that they seem not in the least offended by this sexual traffic of the streets, they look at me as if I were a visitor from Mars. This kind of sexual play is as much a part of everyday life as the baguette at the breakfast, lunch and dinner table and one fears its absence far more than its presence. But what if you don't like the insistence of the gaze or if it's followed by action and you aren't too fond of the person doing the acting? I interrogate the young caretaker of my building. 'Well, I just tell them where to get off, don't I,' she responds, far more outraged at the naïvety of my question than the facts within it; and with a look which tells me that my mother must have failed somewhere in my basic education since I don't seem to have even the most fundamental savvy of street life. Other friends explain patiently that this is not an Anglo-Saxon and puritan country. We are Mediterranean they tell me, come from a Catholic tradition, we have no problems with the body, with sex.

All this trips easily off the tongue and has been noted many times before. However, the context of political correctness brings these differences in the social relations of sexuality into relief in a new way. What has grown clear to me over my months here is that whereas in the American and to a somewhat lesser extent British imagination, sex is now coupled with fear of violence, this is not the case in France. It is not that there is no sexual violence here, no rape or child abuse. The most recent statistics on reported rape show a marked increase in reported rapes over the last five years. There is outrage too at paedophilia rings and child prostitution. But the instant and immediate equation of sex and violence is not made. There is none of that culture of sexual fear which has rendered blue night lights a *sine qua non* of American campuses. Women are not constituted – either by feminists or the media, or the general linguistic usage – in the first instance, as victims of the male threat. The trials which fascinate the public are not primarily those which focus on sexual assault or abuse. Indeed, the two trials which have recently captured imaginations, the *procès* Villemin and the *procès* Cons-Boutboul, feature tough women: the first a mother who may have murdered the child her husband was convicted of murdering; the second a defrauding and altogether bourgeoise grandmother who may have had her interfering son-in-law shot.

Like men, women here are *active* agents on the social

and sexual stage. Penetration – which can so easily slide into rape in current American feminist discourse – is neither a terror nor the single signifying instance which characterises what sex is. Sex is fluid, covering everything from the glance in the street, banter in shops or at table and the pleasures of food to the bedchamber – though it may not have to go so far. This is perfectly acceptable, is, one could say, 'socially correct', is, in fact, the spice of everyday life.

There is no climate in France which makes men, generically, the enemy. During the infamous American Bobbit trial, there was consternation amongst my women friends – who, I should note, are in social terms no different from my British women friends – that the perpetrator of what was considered to be a serious crime should have got off scot-free. When I told my French publisher that my own initial reaction on hearing of Bobbit's castrating act had been to laugh gleefully, she was rather taken aback. 'But it's so violent,' she said. She could, of course, understand the delayed defensive action plea for battered women in general. What she had no immediate place for was my laughter.

French women, it seems, like men. They do not in a generalised, unspecific way feel angry at or anxious about them. So too, it would seem, since feelings rarely run in a single direction, French men like women.

It is no accident that no one is particularly bothered by the countless rumours about President Mitterand's innumerable lovers and illegitimate children. These are neither reported in the press nor seen as a blot on his political honour. The French, I'm constantly told, like their politicians to have 'spunk'. If there is any fault, they go on to say, it is simply that rewards of office may too often go along with the bedchamber. But then, Mitterand has always preferred highly intelligent and capable women, so why not! Sex, for the French, is after all simply part of life, not a touchstone for moral outrage. Nor is it a subject for moral discourse. The French find British and American politicians' resignations on grounds of illicit sexual activity ridiculous.

Pornography, too, provides a telling contrast. There is no particular cult here of slasher films. Late night television has a myriad of what in Britain would be termed soft-porn programmes. These are mostly couched as comedy rather than the melodrama of their American hard-porn counterparts – which come on weekends in the small hours on the cable channels. In French soft porn, women appear as objects of infinite desire; they do a lot of dressing and undressing, while the men chase and more often than not stumble over trousers or bedposts, only to be caught with their socks on. They may be voyeurs, but they are also figures of fun. (Cuckolds, too, we should remember, are in France traditionally figures of comedy, not tragic heroes. It is the women who struggle heroically between duty and passion.) In American porn, its private parts and the hard pleasureless work of sex aside, there is a preponderance of a flimsy plot device which in one way or another builds into the narrative a justification of pornography as a whole. The American logic of guilt, the puritan trap, makes itself felt even in this lowly genre.

It may be provocation to admit it, but I cannot see that the far more easygoing culture of sexuality in France has done women any harm. Laws which enable and protect women are no worse than in Britain, and in certain instances better than in the United States. A law which extended the definition of rape was passed in 1980. The

Learning Resources Centre

law permits various associations (as well as family) to bring a charge on the victim's behalf. Rape is defined as sexual penetration of any kind committed by one person on another by violence, constraint or surprise. Aggravating circumstances include the person's vulnerable state (illness, pregnancy, mental or physical infirmity), status as a minor of 15 or under, threat by arms, gang rape, the infliction of permanent infirmity or any mutilation. In 1989 a law was passed permitting victims of incest to bring a case to court in the ten years following their majority.

After 20 years of feminism – which most women now say is all but dead as a movement – abortion up to eight weeks is available on demand (even if there can be difficulties in finding a clinic in certain regions and women who wait beyond eight weeks find themselves having to go abroad). Since 1992 hindering an abortion is an offence which can be taken to court. In November 1992, sexual harassment in the workplace became a criminal offence. This is defined as an abuse of authority in sexual matters within work relations and includes all sexual blackmail by a superior or a subordinate and carries with it a penalty of up to a year in prison, a fine of up to £85,000, or the payment of damages and interest. If the 'harassed' person has been fired or suffered professionally, and the case is won, reinstatement must follow. (Though it is too early for statistics to speak about the new law, they do show that in 1991 20 per cent of French working women felt that at some time in their careers they had suffered from harassment.[1])

As for laws to do with women as mothers, France's welfare benefits compare well with other countries. All medical charges are covered by the state. Maternity leave allows for six prenatal weeks off work and ten postnatal – more if there are other children at home. The mother's job must be kept for her return to work; and social security, if she doesn't return, is calculated at 84 per cent of her salary. On top of this, up until the child's third year, both mothers and fathers can ask for a year's full-time or part-time leave, twice renewable, to educate their children – and jobs must be kept open for their return.

Pre-school childcare facilities are far more numerous than in Britain. The number of collective crèches, which take babies from three months, has tripled in the last 20 years, while other kinds of facility have risen five times. All forms of childcare for working mothers receive a 25 per cent deduction off income tax on expenses incurred and fees for public institutions are on a sliding scale related to earnings. Most amazingly of all, in the light of the punishing attitude in Britain, single mothers not only take precedence, but also receive additional rebates. France, with its traditional population concerns, one has to remember, has always stressed the welfare of the child and woman as mother above all else. Maternity medals may no longer be awarded, but their equivalent is there in terms of benefits.

As for women in the workplace, statistics for 1990 showed that for the group aged between 25 and 39, 90 per cent of women without children worked; 83 per cent of women with one child; 73 per cent with two children; and 47 per cent with three. In the professions, 55 per cent of all teachers were women; 31 per cent of doctors and 41 per cent of lawyers. In 1993, 61 per cent of all law students were women. Twenty-two per cent of executive functions in France are held by women as against only 10 per cent in Britain; and only 24 per cent of women who work do so part-time, as opposed to 45 per cent in Britain. It goes without saying that the French were scandalised to hear the discriminatory conditions which attended part-time work in Britain until the House of Lords moved in March 1994 to rectify the situation.

As in Britain, women rarely attain the highest posts in business, in the civil service or in politics. Women make up only 5.3 per cent of MPs in France, even trailing behind Britain's 7.7 per cent. Commentators have noted that because the French have never had queens, the idea of a woman acting as a representative of the people, let alone a figure of political power, is still a difficult one. But Edith Cresson, briefly and unhappily prime minister, has said in a recent interview that this is really a problem of a closed and male political class which is suspicious of women and won't let them into the club. '*Machisme*' is prevalent. Then too, it should not be forgotten that French women were not granted the vote until after the Liberation in 1944, and then only because de Gaulle stressed their heroic performance in the resistance. Currently much is being made of the lack of women in politics; the socialist party leader has called for 50 per cent women candidates in the forthcoming European elections. The debate about this is not so very different from the one in Britain, though women in power or on their way to power are quick to say – without any hint that this might be an outlandish confession – that they want to lose nothing either in terms of sexual attractiveness or maternal place. To look well, to be a mother, is a matter here of feminine pride, though it comes as no surprise to hear that women wish for more help from men around the home and with children. And with the pressure from the extreme right to ease unemployment by offering women who stay home a 'maternal wage' equal to the minimum wage, there is certainly a sense amongst women that the gains of the last 20 years must now be staunchly defended if they are not to be eroded.

If PC has not bitten in France because of different underlying attitudes to sexuality, the case holds for race as well. Black people are still called '*noirs*', Blacks, or if immigrants by their department or country of origin, but not hyphenated as '. . . -French'. North Africans, the largest non-European population in France, are generally known as 'Maghrebians', after the region from which they come. Some ten years ago, the word Beurs came into widespread use to designate first-generation Maghrebians. Beur is Verlan – that kind of coded French street slang which humorously reverses the syllables of words – for 'Arab'. North African women are known as Beurettes. The term is a self-chosen one which grew out of the culture of the Arab suburbs and has no slur associated with it.

What is most extraordinary coming here from either Britain or the United States is how little of a culture of offence there exists in questions of race and ethnicity. Heightened liberal sensitivities, soft notions of multiculturalism which make allowances for or even celebrate differences that run counter to established French practices are hardly the order of the day. For instance, no exceptions are made for Islamic girls who want to wear chadors to state schools. Religious schools can be created; but if these want government subsidies, then, apart from some hours devoted to religious education, the national curriculum must still be followed. The principle holds good for Catholic schools, Jewish schools and so on. (France is perhaps the only country in the world where a demonstration to support state, and that means *secular*, education, could muster some 650,000 participants – a procession covering 13 kilometres of Paris streets.)

Little obvious attempt has been made to change the university curriculum so that the sensibilities of Muslims or Blacks are taken into account. During the events surrounding Salman Rushdie and the fifth anniversary of the infamous fatwa, not a single article suggested that Rushdie had called down the wrath of the Ayatollah on himself. Indeed, it was French Muslim intellectuals who put together the first collection of Islamic pro-Rushdie writings in a volume called *Pour Rushdie*.

This is not to say that France is any more (or less) 'racist' than Britain. It is simply that the analysis of ethnic questions is different, as is what can be done to ease race relations. In a recent demonstration by SOS-Racisme (one of several anti-racism organisations) which targeted the new tougher immigration laws, the placards had an unfamiliar ring. '*Un raciste c'est quelqu'un qui se trompe de colère*', trumpeted some: a racist is someone who has found a mistaken object for his anger, or a racist is someone who's made a mistake about colour – punning on the closeness of sound of '*colère*' and '*couleur*'. Racism, in other words, marks a mistake of analysis. Difference is not the primary cause of social ills, though it is difference that is blamed when economy and polity are awry.

Perhaps because of the recent and death-riddled rise of Islamic fundamentalism in its former colony of Algeria, which is only a strip of Mediterranean away, France (and that includes its Maghrebians) has a far less softly liberal attitude towards 'differences' which run counter to enshrined values. Tolerance is, of course, crucial, but there is no tolerance amongst intellectuals and commentators towards intolerance. '*La France ce n'est que des Frances conçues ensemble*' (France is only Frances conceived of together), as the famous and much cited historian Braudel has noted, but all those Frances are staunchly republican and secular.

Some may think it strange, but this tougher attitude has not resulted in greater racial and ethnic friction than in more politically correct climates. One indication of this lies in a recent survey of first-generation Maghrebians between the ages of 19 and 30 – and there are about a million in France – which showed that 71 per cent of those interviewed felt closer to the French way of life and French culture than to the culture of their parents. The degree of integration into French ways rose, not surprisingly, with the level of education. (I should note that integration here is seen as a good both by the majority of Maghrebians and French non-Maghrebians: an American-style culture of rigorous ethnic separateness and splintering is seen to lead logically only to apartheid.) More surprising perhaps, relations between the sexes were a primary form of integration. Sixty-five per cent of the Maghrebian women, 81 per cent of the men, had had sexual relations with French non-Maghrebians. I have no comparative statistics for the Asian population in Britain or comparable groups in America but I imagine that the French figures are high. That this may have as much to do with French ease about sexuality as with the nature of race relations is a given, but the latter must none the less play their part, particularly since only 27 per cent of the sample indicated that they had anything against *marriage* with a non-Maghrebian. Then too, 70 per cent of the sample said they had never been a victim of racism at work; 69 per cent never at school; 64 per cent never from members of the public in the streets, although 60 per cent of the men and 38 per cent of the women said they had suffered from racism in the streets at the hands of the police.

I cannot provide statistics for Blacks along the same lines. That is because figures based on race and ethnicity are not collected by official bodies. (Figures exist for foreigners, but since many immigrants to mainland France are already French nationals, they do not come into these figures.) This is perhaps the only evidence of PC I have found in France, though its expression runs counter to the American trend of particularising populations. Indeed for the past year there has been debate about excising the word race from the Constitution, where it exists with anti-racist intent, since arguments abound to show that the concept of race has no scientific consistency and poses more questions than it answers.

It is interesting to ask oneself why political correctness has taken no hold in France as it has in the United States and Canada and in a lesser way in Britain – always it seems a halfway house between America and the rest of Europe. Many of the conditions after all are similar. France is a sophisticated Western nation with a history of both radicalism and colonialism. It has a mixed ethnic population which features large numbers of former colonials, towards whom the host society shows varying degrees of intolerance. It is concerned with race relations. It has had a strong feminist movement and though as a movement this may for the moment have played itself out, the issue of women's parity has not.

Much of the answer lies, I think, in the nature of the French state. The state in France is a far more powerful and many-tentacled body than in Britain. It is still seen as the creation of a republican and secular revolution which enshrined the values of the Enlightenment and is still largely respected as the upholder of rights: of Liberty, Equality and Fraternity. Sure, some think the police have too little or too much power; or that things have moved too far to the left or the right; but in the birthplace of deconstruction the central narrative of the just state still remains only slightly chipped. The government of the day may have to be petitioned, marched against, overthrown by peaceful or more radical means, so that the state can be made to adhere more fully or more closely to this core idea of justice, but the story of the possible just state is intact. One is a citizen here not by birth, that is by parental line, but by buying into a just culture. Immigrant or ethnic groups may have to battle for their rights, but there is a sense that these may be granted, as long as the central narrative is accepted.

France is a country where the public sphere is still largely intact. There is no mood here of staggering social breakdown. This is still on the whole a unified and homogeneous society in which unspoken as well as spoken rules hold good. People feel – with the usual grumps and groans – that they have and can elect a government that represents them. The traditional sites of collective action, the unions, still function and are far noisier than their British counterparts. Not a week has passed in the last six months without a major demonstration in some part of Paris. As unemployment mounts dramatically and the numbers of homeless increase, these too band together, vociferously sell the newspapers – *Réverbère*, *Faim du Siècle* – which bring them some funds and speak their situation. And though Prime Minister Balladur may not be able to turn round the French economy in a trice, he makes the gestures of compromise which marchers and 'public opinion' demand of him. What all this means is that, unlike America in the Reagan years, the French feel they have a stake in the running of the nation.

In the 1980s America which saw the birth of political correctness, civil society and the public sphere were largely eroded; as they were in Britain during the Thatcher era. With a government which showed little heed for its citizens' welfare, disaffection with national political life set in along with a sense of social breakdown. Out of this a politics of identity arose. The new politics generated new rules – and rules after all are only an attempt to control a world which seems to be spiralling out of control. In that sense, PC with its rule-generating obsession is a direct outgrowth of the Reagan years – indeed its mirror image just slightly out of focus. A twist of the kaleidoscope and Reagan's moral majority become the puritanical rule-making guardians of PC.

In France those years were marked by Mitterand's 'socialist' presidency. Though perhaps now past its due date, this meant that the state was for some years also more open to all conventionally oppositional demands for greater rights and parity. The state, unlike Reagan's America, was, itself, on the side of social claims and a more generous definition of justice. If socialist ideals were not always implemented, Mitterand's court of advisers none the less included many of the radical intellectuals who might otherwise have fired oppositional groups.

These are the same kind of intellectuals who teach in the universities – in America and Britain the seedbeds of political correctness. And the different nature and status of universities and their occupants in France and the Anglo-American countries are significant in this account. If political correctness has not taken root here, it is because institutions of higher learning are valued by politicians and people alike and are influential. They are on the whole large urban conglomerates, not closed campus societies like American Ivy League and liberal arts colleges. Then, too, student life takes place in cafés, which may not necessarily be touchstones of reality, but are at least places peopled not solely by students and academics. The student–staff ratio is huge: students will rarely have the opportunity of meeting a don face to face, let alone behind those doors where sexual fantasy seems to run rife. Paradoxically, the lack of those metaphorical campus walls gives the individual dons both less direct power over students' lives and more power in the society as a whole. Intellectuals in France are part of the public arena and being a student is not a time away from life but a necessary step on one's integration into the rest of life. The universities, and particularly those elite graduate training schools like ENA and the Ecole Normale Supérieure are understood and valued as places where the administrators, leaders, businessmen, scientists and intellectuals of tomorrow are shaped.

I suspect that in America the very distance of the universities from the rest of the social sphere (and the imagined sense of the distance of academic life remains, even when universities are located in cities) is largely responsible for the particular distortions we have seen take place there. Date rape, the confusion about sexual practices and the sets of complex rules put in place to control them, may have something to do with transporting young women from the safety of white middle-class homes to bewildering and hence frightening multiracial and multiclass campuses. Old friends, parents, family are distant and on campus there is a sexual ideology which not only names man as the enemy, but puts in place already indoctrinated care workers, whose careers depend on cases of harassment, rape, and so on, as the first point of call for the bewildered girl. In France, where some of the universities are equally multicultural in their population, students, at least for their first years, often still live at home. And date rape is not an idea that has taken hold.

French friends tell me that PC cannot take root here, not only because of the different nature of the universities, not only because of the lack of a cultural puritanism, but also because an already gendered language doesn't lend itself to politically correct manipulation. Politics, beauty, truth, the republic, are already feminine words. They cite with hilarity French Canadian tamperings with the language: in order to translate English politically correct equalising usage of she and he, the Québecois have had to come up with a '*le personne*' – a monstrous grammatical construct, even to my ears. (Person, in French, is a feminine word.)

I hope they're right – not because there isn't a great deal wrong in France, as the French will also quickly tell you. Despite France's fair laws, gays find life in Britain less stifling. Bureaucracy is rife; the police force is not free of racism, nor is the society as a whole. Life in the multi-ethnic suburbs is very tough indeed. Unemployment is spiralling, particularly amongst the young, and when they, or anyone else, march, the police force is out in the streets in numbers not seen since May 1968.

Whether France's present economic plight and new governments of the right will lead to an erosion of the public sphere and hence a rise in PC is a guess for the prognosticators; as much as whether the United States under President Clinton will see the death of PC. None the less, for the time being, the centre still holds with many of its Enlightenment values and notions of a 'providential' society, as they call the welfare state, in place. And one can still exchange glances in the street without fearing rape.

Then, too, my daughter is making her way through three hundred smelly, runny cheeses. Only occasionally does she think of nice clean cheddar wrapped in plastic with nostalgia.

NOTE

1 All survey details in this piece come from either INSEE, Ministère de Travail, Francoscopie or Cerc.

Stuart Hall

SOME 'POLITICALLY INCORRECT' PATHWAYS THROUGH PC

According to one version, political correctness actually began as an in-joke on the left: radical students on American campuses acting out an ironic replay of the Bad Old Days BS (Before the Sixties) when every revolutionary groupuscule had a party line about everything. They would address some glaring example of sexist or racist behaviour by their fellow students in imitation of the tone of voice of the Red Guards or Cultural Revolution Commissar: 'Not very "politically correct", *Comrade*!' Marx (commenting on how the revolutionaries of one age frequently appeared in the disguise of those of a previous age) once famously remarked that 'History happens twice, the first time as tragedy, the second time as farce.' He forgot to add that, the third time, the joke would almost certainly turn round and bite you.

In fact, the first time I actually encountered the term 'political correctness' was when I was giving a talk at an American university in the mid-1980s. I was warned by the organisers of a conference that I should be careful about what I said because, in the new climate of the times following the Reagan election, the right had established campus committees to monitor speakers and take notes on everything said in lectures which could be interpreted as undermining the American Constitution or sapping the moral fibre of the nation's brightest and best. Here, PC was clearly part and parcel of the 1980s backlash against the 1960s. It was the right and the Moral Majority who were trying to prescribe what could and could not be thought and said in academic classrooms. The experience of the 'thought police' in operation at close quarters was sufficiently unpleasant for me to have, at best, highly ambiguous feelings when political correctness started to be implemented by what one may loosely call 'our side' in defence of what, in most cases, I take to be 'our issues'.

Some extremely odd reversals seemed to be going on here. Strategies associated with the radical right, the security state or the authoritarian left were being appropriated by the inheritors of the free-speech, libertarian radicalism of the 1960s. The only arguments against it seemed to belong to the most feeble of the classical liberal cop-outs. Meanwhile, as a tactic, PC seemed to be empowering small groups of militants in the classrooms and in academic debate about curricula, etc, while leaving them increasingly isolated in the wider political arena. What seemed most characteristic of the PC issue was the way it cut across the traditional left/right divide, and divided some sections of the left from others. In all these ways, PC was and remains prototypical of the kinds of issues which have come to characterise the rapidly shifting political landscape of the 1990s, and thus to be symptomatic of certain broader historical trends. It therefore seems useful, even at this late stage, to place PC in a broader historical context before trying to chart a path through its contradictions.

First, there is the question of its 'Americanness'. My own view is that when people dismiss PC as 'really an American phenomenon', they are thinking about PC in too narrow a way, as well as hoping that labelling it will make it go away. I want to argue that, as a political strategy – even more, as a political *style* – PC was an active presence in British politics in the early 1980s, even though at the time it was known by a different name. What's more, its so-called 'Americanness' tells us something significant about how all post-industrial societies are changing and what is happening to the politics of liberal democratic countries everywhere.

PC seems to me to reflect the fragmentation of the political landscape into separate issues; and the break-up of social constituencies, or at least their refusal to cohere any longer within some broader collective identity or 'master category' like that of 'class' or 'labour'. In fact, PC seems to be typical of those societies where there has been an erosion of the mass party as a political form, a decline in active participation in mass political movements and a weakening in the influence and power of the 'old' social movements of the working class and industrial labour. It has taken hold in places where the political initiative has passed to the 'new social movements', which is of course the soil in which PC has been nurtured. It therefore reflects a seismic shift in the political topography.

In the old days, class and economic exploitation were what the left considered the 'principal contradiction' of social life. All the major social conflicts seemed to flow from and lead back to them. The era of PC is marked by the proliferation of the sites of social conflict to include conflicts around questions of race, gender, sexuality, the family, ethnicity and cultural difference, as well as issues around class and inequality. Issues like family life, marriage and sexual relations, or food, which used to be considered 'non-political', have become politicised. PC is also characteristic of the rise of 'identity politics', where shared social identity (as woman, Black, gay or lesbian), not material interest or collective disadvantage, is the mobilising factor. It reflects the spread of 'the political' from the public to the private arena, the sphere of informal social interaction and the scenarios of everyday life. The feminist slogan, 'The personal is political', captures these shifts perfectly.

On another dimension, PC is a product of what we might call 'the culturing of politics' – an approach which is based on the recognition that our relationship to 'reality' is always mediated in and through language and that language and discourse are central to the operations of power. It is politics 'after cultural studies', in the sense that it has absorbed many of the theoretical developments in cultural theory and philosophy of recent decades. It may not know much economics, but it sure understands that things – including the movements of the economy – only make sense and become the objects of political struggle because of how they are represented. In other words, they have a cultural or discursive dimension. In this sense, we may say that PC arises in an intellectual culture which has undergone what the philosophers call 'the linguistic turn'.

Taken together, these things go some way to explaining the particular *style* of PC: its confrontational, in-your-face mode of address. It consciously intrudes a stance and tone of voice which seem more appropriate to public contestation into so-called 'private' space. Many have commented on the intellectualist or 'academic' nature of PC politics. I think they not only mean that PC often seems to be contained within academia. They are also referring to what some philosophers would call its extreme 'nominalism', that is to say, its apparent belief that if things are called by a different name they will cease to exist. It has a highly individualist notion of politics – politics as the lone, embattled individual 'witnessing to the Truth'. PC gives the impression of a small but dedicated band who are determined to stand up and be counted. That isn't the only sense in which PCers remind one of latter-day Puritans like the Saints of the seventeenth century. A strong strain of moral self-righteousness has often been PC's most characteristic 'voice'.

The rise of political correctness seems to be intimately connected with the fact that, in the US until recently and in the UK still, the 1980s and 1990s have been marked by the dominance of the political new right. The Reagan–Bush and Thatcher regimes commanded the political stage. But they also set the parameters of political action and moral debate. They redefined the contours of public thinking with their virulently free-market social philosophy and set in motion a powerful, new, anti-welfare consensus. Their ascendancy was built not only on their command of the whole state apparatus of government but also on their mastery of the ideological terrain – their willingness to address ideological questions like morality, sexuality, parenting, education, authority in the classroom, traditional standards of learning, the organisation of knowledge in the curriculum – with the seriousness which they deserved. They successfully fashioned a seductive appeal to selfishness, greed and possessive individualism, striking a sort of populist alliance across the lines of traditional class alignments and introducing the gospel that 'market forces must prevail' into the very heart of the left's traditional support. They exploited ordinary people's basic fears of crime, race, 'otherness', of change itself. They fished in the murky waters of a narrow and reactionary cultural nationalism and rallied around their sexual and cultural agenda a highly vocal and well-organised 'silent' Moral Majority. Paradoxically, though PC is its sworn adversary, the New Right shares with PC an understanding that the political game is often won or lost on the terrain of these moral and cultural issues, apparently far removed from the Westminster (or for that matter, Labour's) conception of 'politics'.

In Britain, despite the cosmetic shift to the more acceptable face of 'Majorism', nothing has been able to derail the long-term, historic transformation of British society which Thatcherism initiated. It is important to distinguish here between an effective mastery of political power in government, of which we have seen many examples, and the project of the New Right, which represents something deeper and more profound. We are talking about the use of political power in order to 'wind up' one whole historical era – the welfare-state, Keynesian, full-employment, comprehensive education-era on which the postwar settlement was constructed – and its replacement by another entirely new type of social order. Its outlook penetrated deep into social, moral, sexual and family life. It has more or less comprehensively transformed all our public institutions – forcing them, through the application of new principles of enterprise management, either to directly obey or indirectly to 'mimic' the market. It has a philosophy, a recipe for everything: for remodelling not only how we behave as citizens and voters, but as mothers, fathers, children, teachers, doctors and lovers.

This deep-seated, multifaceted, fundamental programme of 'reform' was put in motion by the conduct of a new kind of politics: a political struggle conducted on many different fronts at the same time, with an intellectual, a moral, a cultural and a philosophical cutting edge, as well as an economic strategy. Its success is to be judged not just by its capacity to win elections, albeit on a minority basis, but by its effectiveness in remaking public and civic life. Despite its commitment to 'roll back the state', its triumph lay in the management of society in its most minute detail – from whether the gift by private charities of hot soup to the homeless was likely to make them more 'dependent', to whether or not it is acceptably 'British' to cheer the West Indies cricket team when it is knocking the stuffing out of the English side at Lords. The conduct of politics on the basis of the mastery of a range of different struggles, the welding together of different interests into a broad populist 'alliance' and the capacity not just to reflect a consensus but to 'win consent', to construct a majority out of a series of minorities, makes it appropriate to call the New Right's strategic conduct of politics 'hegemonic'.

That, precisely, has been the weakness of the traditional left, at least in the UK. Its response to this New Right offensive has been defensive, retreating to its well-defined, but increasingly obsolescent and declining sources of strength. It has failed to engage the new contradictions which the changes have produced, or to rethink its traditional values and commitments in the light of rapidly and permanently changing circumstances. Driven back all along the front, with its philosophy unhinged by wider historical shifts (like the break up of the so-called 'state socialist' experiments in Eastern Europe and the decline of welfare capitalism in the West), the opposition has not been able to stage, let alone win, any engagement of sufficient depth or historical significance to interrupt the right's project. Instead, it has been driven on to the defensive. In particular, it has failed to connect the older forces of reform with any of the newer forces – the new social movements – which we argued earlier are emerging in and characteristic of the more fragmented political landscape we now inhabit.

The GLC was one of the key examples of this in the UK, and is worth recalling here because it helps us to situate PC in the British context. The Ken Livingstone GLC was significant, not only because it represented almost the only serious political alternative to Thatcherism in the 1980s, but because of the new form of politics and political alliances through which it was constituted. In the reconstructed GLC, the 'new' social movements took command within the institutions and in an (often difficult) alliance with the 'old' forces of London Labour and the older culture of Labourism. Following its example, a new kind of 'new left' emerged in several cities. Wherever it was able to win electoral power, it used its position and such funds as it had available (which, for peculiar historic reasons we won't go into, were substantial in the GLC case) to legislate into existence not only an expansion of local services to the poorer parts of the population, but a new kind of anti-sexist, anti-racist, anti-homophobic agenda. This was especially the case in education and in the adoption of equal opportunities and sexual harassment codes which it was able to push through in those areas which still remained under local authority control.

There was something quite novel about this political movement and formation: partly because of the different radical traditions and forces which it brought into alliance; partly because the claims of the new social movements had never before in the UK been within reach of actual policy implementation on this scale. It was also significant, in my view, because the issues were put together in such a way as to cut across the traditional class alignments and create a new kind of potentially popular social 'block'. To put it in terms of our earlier argument, the GLC/local socialism alliance began to look like the only 'hegemonic' political strategy on the left capable of matching, in depth, complexity and novelty, the radical thrust of Thatcherism's project at the national level.

The famous 'fare's fair' campaign on London Transport was paradigmatic. Here was an issue about prioritising public needs over private ones (taking head-on the key Thatcherite theme of privatisation), combined with a strong redistributive and egalitarian emphasis (those who didn't have cars deserved to travel safely and conveniently as much as private car owners), which was linked to some key 'cultural' themes (the revival of urban life and space, environmental damage, the Londoners' pride in the city) and underpinned by an explicitly 'new social movement' theme (the guarantee of safe travel for women and the right of single women to move on their own through the city at their choice at any time of the day or night – the feminist slogan of 'reclaim the night').

It has always seemed to me that destruction of the GLC and the intensity of the assault on local government were motivated by the Thatcher government's desire to strangle in its bed what they unconsciously recognised as a potentially popular and effective new alliance of social forces. And so they did. This attack was spearheaded by the most virulent campaign by the Tory tabloid press about 'loony-left councils' and the proliferation of stories in the media about the banning of 'Baa, Baa, Black Sheep' in schools by over-energetic anti-racist teachers, etc. This vicious campaign was less easy to counter because, as always happens, there was just enough truth in the stories in a few instances to sustain the media amplification. As has become customary since, one found oneself then, as one finds oneself with PC now, fighting on several fronts at once: defending the importance of the issues raised; trying to unmask the politically motivated media hype; while at the same time distancing oneself from some of the undeniable idiocies committed in the name of 'anti-racism' or 'anti-sexism' or 'anti-homophobia' by the militants. Our enemies are bad enough; God save us from our friends.

The rights and wrongs of the GLC-loony-left affair are not worth arguing over, but the deeper political judgements are. What seemed to have happened in the aftermath of Thatcherism's success in rolling back this attempt to legislate the agendas of the new social movements into place was the isolation of these minorities as the political tide receded. The sense of isolation was compounded by a sort of desperate 'triumph of the will' – the determination to stand fast, hold out and press on, even when the wave of popular support which, at an earlier stage, had appeared to be moving its way, ebbed. Perhaps inevitably, what began in the early 1980s as a broad, national-popular strategy of a hegemonic kind – advancing on several fronts at once, combining power in office with an educative approach to politics outside, winning consent and enlarging its popular-democratic base as it went – reverted, in the late 1980s and 1990s, to an older form of politics – a sort of defensive vanguardism.

Now it may be argued that, in fact, a popular-democratic counter-politics to Thatcherism, based around the local socialism/new social movements alliance, was never on the cards. But even if this is true, the consequences of the new social movements, with their novel political agenda and their instinctive understanding of the new political world, reverting from a 'hegemonic' to a vanguardist style of political opposition, has to be reckoned with. It is not only possible but necessary, in my view, to be 'strategic', both when you are advancing and when you are retreating. And no one knows or illustrates that lesson better than the Thatcherite New Right, which has time and again since 1979 been forced back on a defensive holding operation for a time, only to come back fighting on another version of the same, deep strategic vision. When, for example, the NHS proved to be the nation's sticking point in Thatcherism's modernisation programme, Thatcherism did not give up its strategic objective. Instead it sent Mrs T out in front to declare 'It is safe in our hands' – and then set about dismantling its underlying principle by obliging it to submit to market forces, all the while insisting through the weasel words of ministers like Mrs Bottomley that nothing whatsoever had changed. That is what I call advancing strategically while retreating.

I believe, then, that, in the UK, the narrowness, moralism and entrenched vanguardism so characteristic of the recent style of much of PC in the public-political arena was bred in or reinforced by that moment of defeat in the mid-1980s; just as it has been underpinned, elsewhere, by an equivalent, though no doubt different, failure or weakness of the left in the face of the New Right. I would add that what is at issue here is not a tactical judgement about whether the new social movements performed well or badly in this or that particular instance, but a deeper question of how the left should think about political strategy. Can the historic agenda of the new right (which I happen to believe is not simply to stay in power for ever but to reconstruct the whole social and moral-political order irrevocably) be effectively opposed or defeated by a 'vanguardist' minority strategy? My answer to that (which at least has the virtue of consistency) is no. Not only because of the kind of assessment of the historic character of the new right I have tried to make elsewhere but because, as Antonio Gramsci, to whom we owe the concept of politics as a struggle for 'hegemony', once argued, in liberal-democratic societies like ours, politics have irrevocably shifted from what he called (using the military metaphors of the First World War) a 'war of manoeuvre' to a 'war of position'.

A 'war of manoeuvre' is one in which you try to overrun

the opposition forces by frontal assault. A 'war of position' is where you advance on a number of different positions at once, your overall strength residing not in the Walls of Jericho collapsing but in the overall 'balance of forces' across the whole terrain of struggle. The latter is appropriate to societies where power is no longer concentrated in one place or centre, like the Post Office or Government House, which at one time revolutionaries were anxious to seize, but has been dispersed or de-centred across society as a whole. It is also appropriate to a situation, such as is common to all post-industrial societies like ours, where power is exercised not only in the state but in what Gramsci called 'civil society' – yes, precisely through those sites like the culture, moral and social questions, the family, education, religion, gender, sexuality, race, national identity, the media, religion, which, we argued earlier, the new social movements and the 'culturing of politics' have brought into the centre of the political equation. Though effective defence is an essential part of modern political struggles, and winning power is an important element, they are no substitute for a strategic form of politics pursued as a 'war of position'.

Another key point in this 'war of position' kind of strategy is that it prioritises 'winning consent' – winning the majority over to your side – over simply 'winning battles'. It is conscious that, in the aftermath of liberal democracy, however limited those gains of universal suffrage, free speech, the rule of law, may now appear to be, the decisive engagements will be fought out over what we might call 'democratic' terrain. That is to say, anyone who is seriously in the business of the long-term transformation of society into something better has to come to terms with the awkward fact that we live after – i.e. 'post'

– the democratic revolution. The question of winning the majority cannot be sacrificed to our own purist sense of being 'correct' for that simply leads to being 'lefter than thou', to thinking that the minority knows best and will, if necessary, force the majority to be free.

That was the defence of the Leninist version of the 'war of manoeuvre'; and we can see in Eastern Europe today some of the consequences of its vanguardism (e.g. a revolutionary change which failed to win, educate and transform 'the majority', who simply bided their time, and have since reverted to many of the archaic, ethnocentric, racist and nationalistic attitudes they held before the Leninists seized power 'on their behalf'). A war of position cannot afford for a moment, in the name of some 'Higher Good' or some 'superior knowledge', to free itself of the harsh discipline of democracy. Unless it is coupled with a strategy which is democratic – in the sense that it genuinely addresses the real fears, confusions, the anxieties as well as the pleasures of ordinary people, tries to educate them to new conceptions of life, to win them over and thus to constitute majorities where there are now only fragmented minorities – it is destined to fail in the long run, whatever its little local successes. The result of pushing *Jenny Lives with Eric and Martin* for distribution in local schools through an education committee on a narrow majority without the hard graft of winning parents to a less homophobic view of sexuality, may only be to make the backlash, when it comes, that bit more extreme, even though at the time the victory over the bigots may make the saving remnant feel good. This is a hard truth which, paradoxically, it seems to me the forces of PC in its post-GLC manifestation and the traditional Labour Party, in their different ways, have signally failed to grasp.

The principal deduction I make, then, from the attempt to place PC in some kind of longer political and historical perspective, is that it is a vanguardist tactic pursued as if it could yield strategic political results. Correct in taking these wider cultural and social issues on board, it has no proper understanding of the centrality of an 'educative' conception of politics, and of the winning of consent to the effective pursuit of the 'culture wars'. It has radicalised the political agenda, but it is stuck in an old and discredited conception of 'the political'.

The political assessment is, however, only the start of the story. We need to go on to question some of PC's fundamental, underlying assumptions, especially as these appear in its post-GLC, post-mid-1980s manifestation. Such an assessment is not easy to make, and although my overall judgement is negative there are some anti-PC arguments which seem to me invalid, requiring a more balanced and nuanced account of its strengths and weaknesses. For example, the old left critique – that PC concerns itself with irrelevant and trivial issues as compared with the 'real' questions of poverty, unemployment and economic disadvantage which it ought to be addressing – is patently unacceptable. It is the product of an archaic view, a sort of crass, low-flying materialism, that 'class' is both more real and more simple to address than, say, gender; that 'class', because it is linked to the economic, is somehow more materially determining, and that the economic factors work as it were on their own, outside of their social and ideological, their gendered and 'raced' conditions of existence. This seems to me absolutely wrong; and clinging to it is representative of the way in which, despite everything that has happened in the last three decades to disturb or challenge its assumptions, a traditionalist conception of 'left politics' remains rock solid and deeply embedded in the collective consciousness (even, surprisingly, among some committed feminists!).

PCers are surely correct in foregrounding the neglected questions of gender, sexuality, race, ethnicity, language, knowledge, the curriculum, the ethnocentricity of the canon and so on. If so, then they are also correct in trying to make them the objects of political struggle. They are also surely correct in saying that the reason why 'politics' has traditionally neglected these questions is not through some conscious, rational choice or conspiracy to do so but because the whole culture works so as to render these social antagonisms politically invisible. That being the case, it will – as PC rightly argues – take a good deal of stomping around, the tumbling of sacred taboos, the breaking of collusive silences, even to render these issues visible – let alone think up institutional strategies, which might address them effectively. What's more, if policy and institutional changes are made which don't penetrate to the level of personal practice in everyday life, the changes won't in the end matter. We all know right-on anti-sexist men who are so busy passing equal opportunities resolutions through their workplaces they just can't spare a moment to do the washing up.

On the other hand, PC should know that challenging the assumptions built into our ordinary use of language is one thing, policing language is another. Trying to get people collectively to change their behaviour towards minorities is one thing and telling them what they can and can't do is something altogether different. It knows, or should know that if the way we practise politics doesn't succeed in 'winning identification' it cannot produce the new political subjects who must actually sustain the practice, no matter how 'objectively' correct the analysis. What we call identities are not created outside of culture and then mobilised by politics. Instead, politics consists fundamentally of the process of forming individuals (whose identities are multiple and divided) into 'new political subjects' (i.e. making people with a whole range of skin colours feel and act 'Black' politically; making a variety of different women 'feminist' in their thinking) and winning their identification (which will never be total or homogeneous) to certain political positions. A strategy designed to silence problems without bringing them out and dealing with them is dealing with difficult issues at the level of symptom rather than cause.

The problem with PC, then, in my view, does not lie with its agenda, with which I sometimes agree, but with its failure to grasp the implications of the positions which it appears to hold. Anyone who understands the importance of language knows that meaning cannot be finally fixed because language is by its very nature multi-accentual, and meaning is always on the slide. It is the right which wishes to intervene ideologically in the infinite multi-accentuality of language and tries to fix it in relation to the world so that it can only mean one thing – roughly, whatever it is John Patten has decided in his infinite wisdom young people need to be taught in order to become proper little English men and women. However, the idea that, by a process of legislation the left can or should intervene to try to fix language is simply to play exactly the same game as John Patten, only upside down or back-to-front. But one of the major lessons we have learned since 'the linguistic turn' in philosophy and cultural theory is that you do not escape from the effects of a model or a practice simply by turning it on its head.

To believe that *all* Black people are good and clever may be a relief after centuries in which they have been thought to be nasty, brutish and dumb; but it is still predicated on racist assumptions. One needs to give up on trying to secure an anti-racist politics on biological or genetic grounds, whether the latter are working for us or for the National Front. The real break comes not from inverting the model but from breaking free of its limiting terms, changing the frame.

PC has changed what it wants the language and the culture to say and mean but it has not changed its conception of how meaning and the culture *work*. This is not only a question of language. The whole PC strategy depends on a conception of politics as the unmasking of false ideas and meanings and replacing them by true ones. It is erected in the image of 'politics as truth' – a substitution of the false racist or sexist or homophobic consciousness by a 'true consciousness'. It refuses to take on board the profound observation (for example, by Michel Foucault and others) that the 'truth' of knowledge is always contextual, always constructed within discourse, always connected with the relations of power which make it true – in short, a 'politics of truth'. The view that we need to struggle over language because discourse has effects for both how we perceive the world and our practice in it, which is right, is negated by the attempt to short-circuit the process of change by legislating some Absolute Truth into being. What's more, what is being legislated is another single, homogeneous truth – our truth to replace theirs – whereas the really difficult task now is to try to hold fast to some perspective of changing the world, making it a better place, while *accepting and negotiating difference*. The last thing we need is the model of one authority substituting one set of identities or truths with another set of 'more correct' ones. The critique of cultural authority, of essentialism and of uniform and homogeneous conceptions of cultural identity have rendered this essentialist conception of politics null and void.

Political correctness, then, is a paradox – which no doubt explains why I feel so deeply ambivalent about it. In one sense, it seems to belong to and to share some of the characteristics of the new political moment. It even seems, at times, to embody some of its new conceptions. At the same time, a great deal of what actually passes for 'PC' in practice is a sort of deformation – a caricature – of a new form of politics. It has been produced by a new political conjuncture. But it does not seem to understand the forces and ideas which have actually produced it. Instead, it tries to conduct new struggles with ancient and decrepit weapons.

The sense we had that PC has divided the left against itself, is not, in the end, an illusion or a mistake because, indeed, there *is* a fundamental divide. This is the divide between, on the one hand, those who believe that politics consists of getting 'our side' where 'their side' used to be, and then exercising power in exactly the same way they did. This binary strategy of governing society by 'policing' it will be justified because it is our side which is doing it. On the other hand, there are those who believe the task of politics in a post-industrial society at a postmodern moment is to unsettle permanently all the configurations of power, preventing them – right or left – from ever settling again into that unconsciousness, the 'deep sleep of forgetfulness', which power so regularly induces and which seems to be a condition of its operation. Along this frontier, I'm afraid, PC falls irredeemably on what I consider to be the wrong side.

Not that I expect the politically correct to agree. Indeed, as I write, I can hear the thumbscrews being unpacked, the guillotine sharpened, the pages of the Dictionary of Political Correctness being shuffled, the tumbrils beginning to roll . . .

NOTES ON THE CONTRIBUTORS

Yasmin Alibhai-Brown was born in Uganda and came as a refugee to Britain in 1972. Having obtained an M. Phil. in English from Oxford University, she then worked in adult education. Since 1982 she has been a journalist, writer and broadcaster specialising in race and cultural issues. She has published in a variety of newspapers and magazines including the *New Statesman & Society*, *Guardian*, *Independent* and *European*. She is also author of several books, including *The Colour of Love* (Virago,

1992). An autobiographical account, *No Place Like Home*, is forthcoming from Virago.

John Annette was born in the USA and came to Britain in 1972 to do postgraduate work at the London School of Economics and Political Science. He is currently Head of the School of History and Politics at Middlesex University, and his research and publications are in the areas of intellectual history, the history of political thought and the history of academic disciplines.

Lisa Appignanesi is a novelist and writer and former Deputy Director of London's Institute of Contemporary Arts. Her recent books include *Freud's Women* (Virago paperback) with John Forrester, and the novels *Dreams of Innocence* and *Memory and Desire* (HarperCollins).

Deborah Cameron teaches linguistics at Strathclyde University, Glasgow; she has also taught at colleges in England and in the USA. She is the author of *Feminism and Linguistic Theory* (Macmillan, 1992), and of the forthcoming study *Verbal Hygiene* (Routledge, 1995).

Linda Grant was born in Liverpool in 1951. She read English at the University of York and did further postgraduate work in Canada. Her first non-fiction work, *Sexing the Millennium: A Political History of the Sexual Revolution*, was published in 1993 and her first novel, *The Cast Iron Shore*, will be published by Picador in 1995. She is a regular contributor to the *Guardian* and *Independent on Sunday*. Her reports on rape in Bosnia have appeared in a number of publications in Britain and abroad.

Stuart Hall was born in Jamaica in 1932. He came to Britain as a Rhodes Scholar at Oxford in 1951 and has been here ever since. A founder-editor of the *New Left Review* in the 1960s, he was for many years Director of the Centre for Cultural Studies at the University of Birmingham. He has written extensively on questions of the media, race and politics in addition to cultural and social theory. His essays during the 1980s tracking Thatcherism were collected in *The Hard Road to Renewal: Thatcherism and the Crisis of the Left* (1988). His current work is on cultural difference, race and ethnicity in 'global times'.

Christopher Hitchens is British, living in America. He writes the Cultural Elite column for *Vanity Fair* and the Minority Report column for the *Nation*. His most recent book is *For the Sake of Argument* (Verso).

Lisa Jardine is Professor of English and Dean of the Faculty of Arts at Queen Mary and Westfield College, University of London. She is the author of *Still Harping on Daughters: Women and Drama in the Age of Shakespeare* (1993), and *Erasmus, Man of Letters: The Construction of Charisma in Print*, (1993). She writes regularly for a number of newspapers and presents the BBC radio 3 programme, *Nightwaves*.

Melanie Phillips is a columnist on the *Observer*. Previously for sixteen years she worked for the *Guardian* as a social services correspondent, social policy leader writer, news editor and columnist. In the mid-80s she wrote a play about anti-semitism called *Traitors* and a book about women in Westminster.

Meera Syal's parents emigrated from New Delhi to England in 1960. She was born and brought up in the West Midlands, and graduated with joint first class honours degrees in English and Drama from Manchester University. As an actress, she has worked extensively in both theatre and television, including seasons at the Royal Court and National Theatre, and created many roles in new plays including Jacinta Condor in Caryll Churchill's *Serious Money* and Anita in Barrie Keefe's *My Girl* and has written and performed her own comic creations in four series of the BBC's 'The Real McCoy'. As a writer, her credits include *A Nice Arrangement* (Cannes and New York Film Festivals), 'My Sister Wife' (Screen Two, winner CRE Award Best TV Drama, nomination Best Screenplay, Writers' Guild) and in 1994 her first feature film, *Bhaji On the Beach*. She was recently named Cosmopolitan Woman of the Year in the Performing Arts. She is married with a young daughter and lives in East London.